Tipbook
Electric Guitar
and Bass Guitar

The Complete Guide

Hugo Pinksterboer

Tipbook
Electric Guitar
and Bass Guitar
The Complete Guide

HAL•LEONARD®

The Complete Guide to Your Instrument!

First edition published in 2002 by
The Tipbook Company bv, The Netherlands

Third edition published in 2008 by
Hal Leonard Books
An Imprint of Hal Leonard Corporation
7777 West Bluemound Road
Milwaukee, WI 53213

Trade Book Division Editorial Offices
19 West 21st Street, New York, NY 10010

Printed in the United States of America

Book design by Gijs Bierenbroodspot

Library of Congress Cataloging-in-Publication Data

Pinksterboer, Hugo.
  Tipbook electric guitar and bass guitar : the complete guide /
Hugo Pinksterboer. — 3rd ed.
     p. cm.
Includes bibliographical references and index.
ISBN 978-1-4234-4274-5
1. Electric guitar. 2. Bass guitar. I. Title.
ML1015.G9P547 2008
787.87'19—dc22
                                    2008044529

www.halleonard.com

Thanks

For their information, their expertise, their time, and their help we'd like to thank the following musicians, teachers, technicians, and other guitar and bass experts:

Elliot Freedman, Stephen White (Guitar Tech, CA), Anderson Page (Modulus Guitars, CA), Wouter Zimmerman (Electric Sound), Henny van Ochten (Texas & Tweed), John van der Veer, Keith Brawley (Brawley Guitars, CA), Ron Knotter, Will Vermeer, Davina Cowan, Mark Zandveld, Gerard Braun, Wim Dijkgraaf, the late Willy Heijnen, Jos Kamphuis, Heino Hoekema, Frans van Ingen, Jean Zijta, Edwin Dijkman and Sander Ruijg, Harm van der Geest, Chris Teerlink and Martin van de Lucht (Luthiers Guitars), Anno Galema, Ulbo de Sitter, Harold Koenders and Tom Keverkamp, Harry de Jonge and everyone else at Sacksioni Guitars, the guitar specialists at Vox Humana, Jean Zijta, and Lex Horst. We also wish to thank Ron Knotter for his musical help in making the Tipcode videos, and Gerard Braun for his invaluable contributions to the Tipbook Chord Diagrams.

About the Author

Journalist, writer, and musician **Hugo Pinksterboer**, author of The Tipbook Series, has published hundreds of interviews, articles, and reviews for national and international music magazines.

About the Designer

Illustrator, designer, and musician **Gijs Bierenbroodspot** has worked as an art director for a wide variety of magazines and has developed numerous ad campaigns. While searching in vain for information about saxophone mouthpieces, he got the idea for this series of books on music and musical instruments. He is responsible for the layout and illustrations for all of the Tipbooks.

Acknowledgments

Cover photo: René Vervloet
Editor: Robert L. Doerschuk and Laura Sassano
Proofreader: Nancy Bishop

Anything missing?

Any omissions? Any areas that could be improved? Please go to www.tipbook.com to contact us, or send an email to info@tipbook.com. Thanks!

Contents

VII

Introduction

Do you plan to buy an electric guitar or a bass, or do you want to learn more about the one you already have? If so, this book will tell you all you need to know. You'll learn about the parts of the instrument and what they do, about lessons and practicing; about auditioning and play-testing guitars and basses; about pickups, strings, picks, and straps; about tuning and maintenance; about the instrument's history and family — and much more.

Having read this Tipbook, you'll be able to get the most out of your instrument, to buy the best (bass) guitar you can, and to easily grasp any other literature on the subject, from books and magazines to online publications.

The first four chapters

If you have just started playing, or haven't yet begun, pay particular attention to the first four chapters. They explain the basics of electric guitars and basses, and they inform you on learning to play the instrument, practicing, and buying or renting a (bass) guitar. This information in these chapters also fully prepares you to read the rest of the book.

Advanced players

Advanced players can skip ahead to Chapter 5, where you find everything you need to know to make an informed choice when you're going to buy a guitar or a bass, introducing you to the

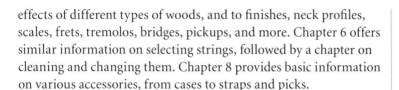

effects of different types of woods, and to finishes, neck profiles, scales, frets, tremolos, bridges, pickups, and more. Chapter 6 offers similar information on selecting strings, followed by a chapter on cleaning and changing them. Chapter 8 provides basic information on various accessories, from cases to straps and picks.

Tuning and maintenance
Two chapters are dedicated to the art of tuning and maintaining your instrument, including both basic and advanced tuning and intonation tips — so don't skip these pages.

Background information
The final four chapters offer background information on the history, the family, the production and the main makers of the instrument.

And more
The glossary and index turn this book into a handy reference, and information on additional resources on the instrument can be found on pages 191 to 196. As another extra, the book provides two pages for essential notes on your equipment.

Street prices
Please note that all prices mentioned in this book are based on estimated street prices in US dollars. Some products may be available for even less money by the time you read this book; others may have become more expensive.

Chord diagrams
Many readers of earlier editions of this Tipbook asked us to include chord diagrams — and so we did. True: This information is also available online, but a book is easier to take along (and you don't have to turn it on either). So here they are. Enjoy!

— Hugo Pinksterboer

See and Hear What You Read with Tipcodes

www.tipbook.com

In addition to the many illustrations on the following pages, Tipbooks offer you a new way to see — and even hear — what you are reading about. The Tipcodes that you will come across throughout this book provide instant access to short movies, sound files, and other additional information at www. tipbook.com.

Here's how it works: Pages 111–113 of this book deal with fitting new strings. On page 113 you'll find **Tipcode EGTR-009**. Type in that code on the Tipcode page at www.tipbook.com, and you will see a short movie on how to put a new string on your guitar. Similar video examples are available on a variety of subjects; other Tipcodes will link to a sound file.

TIPCODE

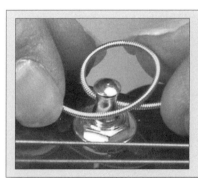

Tipcode EGTR-009
This Tipcodes shows you how to put on a new string.

Quick start

The Tipcode movies and sound files typically start within seconds.
If you miss something the first time, you can of course repeat
them. And if it all happens too fast, use the pause button below the
movie window.

Tipcode list

For your convenience, all the Tipcodes used in this book are
shown in a single list on page 189.

Plug-ins

If the software you need to use the Tipcodes is not yet installed on
your computer, you'll automatically be told which software you

First, make your selection:
Tipcode, chords and
fingering charts, or the
glossary.

The Tipcode window displays
videos, fingering charts, chords,
and explanations of the words
used in this book.

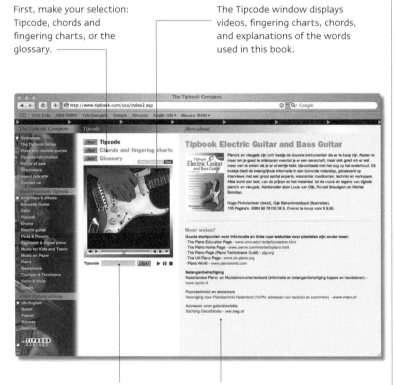

Enter a Tipcode here and click
on the button. Want to see it again?
Click again.

These links take you directly to
other interesting sites.

XIII

need, and where to download it. This kind of software (plug-ins) is free.

Still more at www.tipbook.com

You can find even more information at www.tipbook.com. For instance, you can look up words in the glossaries of all the Tipbooks published to date. For guitarists and pianists there are chord diagrams and for saxophonists, clarinetists, and flutists there are fingering charts, for drummers there are the rudiments. Also included are links to some of the websites mentioned in the *Want to Know More?* section of each Tipbook.

1

Guitarists, Bassists?

Guitarists can play anything from scorching solos and power chords to the sweetest notes and smoothest harmonies. Bassists can slap or pop their instruments, or make them growl or sing just as easily. And both guitarists and bassists are indispensable musicians in many, many styles of music.

With an electric guitar or bass you can play numerous musical styles. From heavy metal to surf, from country to R&B, Cajun or klezmer, folk, jazz, funk, Latin, soul, and even classical music.

One or more

You can concentrate on one style, or you can play as many different types of music as you like.

And you can do so using a single instrument only, or you can find yourself a different one for each type of sound: There are hundreds of different guitars and basses available, each with its own character.

As different as can be

If you would compare a heavy rock guitarist to a jazz guitarist, you'll see more differences than similarities. They use different

Two guitars – as different as can be.

2

types of instruments, different strings, different playing techniques, different amplifiers, different effects — and most probably different picks too.

Bassists too

The same goes for bassists. Some types of music ask for bright, percussive, complex bass patterns, while other bands require no more than a subdued low note on every beat. And there are plenty of different instruments available to suit every need and style. This book helps you make a well-informed purchase.

Chords

Just like keyboard instruments, guitars allow you to play multiple notes simultaneously (*chords*), or play the melody as well as the accompaniment. This turns the instrument into a one-piece band.

Singers

Guitarists often write most of the songs of the band's repertoire, especially if they happen to be the lead singer as well.

Accompaniment

There are plenty of singing bassists too, including artists such as Paul McCartney, Jack Bruce, Sting, Lemmy Kilmister, and Brian Wilson. Most bass players, however, mainly focus on building a solid foundation for the band, closely cooperating with the drummer.

Popular instruments

Electric guitars and basses are popular instruments, in part because they're pretty easy to get started on. With just a little bit of talent and determination, you can play your first songs within a couple of weeks.

Affordable

Because they're so popular and so many of them are made, (bass) guitars are quite affordable. For some three hundred dollars or even less you can get yourself a *gig rig* including an instrument, a small amplifier, a tuner, and everything else you need to start playing.

3

Reading music

The guitar and the bass are also popular instruments because you don't need to read music to get started — and there are lots of guitarists and bassists who can't read a note. Still, it's good to know that reading music isn't that hard to learn. Read more on page 25–26.

For all ages

One more great point about the instrument is that you can start playing at pretty much any age — and you can continue to play forever. For the very youngest players, special downsized guitars are available too. There's more on those instruments on page 56. Have fun!

2

A Quick Tour

This chapter introduces you to the key parts of electric guitars, basses, and also offers a brief introduction to amps and effects.

Acoustic guitars have a large soundbox that amplifies the vibrations of the strings. For the electric instruments in this book, you need an 'electric' amplifier.

Pickups

Electric guitars and basses have *pickups*. These devices literally 'pick up' the strings' vibrations and convert them to electric signals. A cable transports the signals to the amplifier. The amplifier boosts these signals and sends them to the speakers.

Solid bodies

Most electric guitars and basses are *solid-body* instruments: They have a solid body, as opposed to the large, hollow soundbox of an acoustic guitar.

SOLID-BODY ELECTRICS

Solid-body guitars and basses come in an endless variety of shapes and sizes, as you will see in the following chapters.

Pickguard

On many instruments, a *pickguard* protects the body from being scratched by your pick. It also covers the wiring inside the instrument. Solid-body guitars without a pickguard have one or more cover plates on the back.

Neck and headstock

The instrument's strings run along the *neck*, from the body to the *headstock*.

Truss rod

Hidden inside the neck is an adjustable truss rod that helps counteract the tension of the strings. Some necks have other reinforcements as well.

Fingerboard

The front side of the neck is the *fingerboard* onto which you press

6

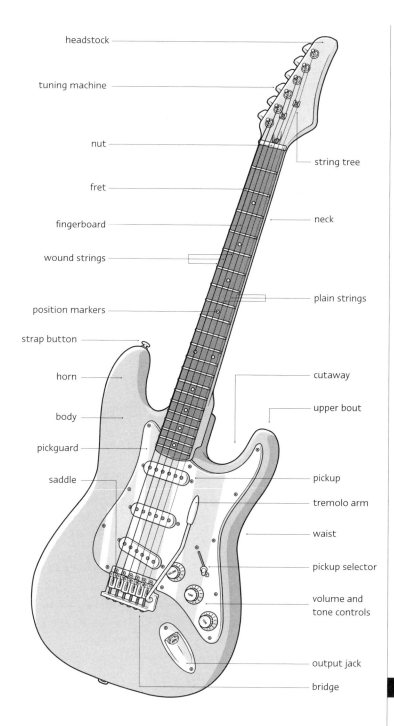

headstock

tuning machine

nut

fret

fingerboard

wound strings

position markers

strap button

horn

body

pickguard

saddle

string tree

neck

plain strings

cutaway

upper bout

pickup

tremolo arm

waist

pickup selector

volume and
tone controls

output jack

bridge

7

your fingers. Pressing a string onto the fingerboard makes the vibrating section of the string shorter. As a result, it will sound higher. This way, you can make any string produce various notes.

Frets

The fingerboard is divided into *positions* by a number of small metal strips, the *frets*. This explains the fingerboard's alternative name, fretboard.

Position markers

Position markers show you where you are at the fingerboard. Most instruments have *side dots* or *side fret markers* as well. These are located on the upper side of the fingerboard, so they're easier to see when you're playing.

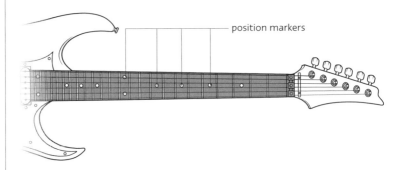

position markers

Fretting strings

Stopping or *fretting* a string in the fifth position is commonly known as playing the string *at the fifth fret.*

Cutaway

To make the highest frets easier to play, most instruments have a *cutaway*: The body is recessed where it meets the neck. Many guitars and basses have a double cutaway, and thus two *horns.*

Waist

Guitar bodies have hips (the *lower bout*) and shoulders (the *upper bout*). In between is the *waist*, which can be either symmetrical or offset.

A solid-body bass guitar with a double cutaway.

Binding

Instruments with an *arched top* often have a decorative and protective strip running along the edges of the body. This *binding* sometimes extends to the neck and the headstock as well.

STRINGS

Most guitars have six strings; most basses have four.

E, A, D, G, B, E

If you start at the thickest, lowest string, the six guitar strings are tuned to the notes E, A, D, G, B, E.

Memory joggers

This sequence can be easily memorized as Eating And Drinking

Give Brain Energy, Eating And Drinking Gives Belly Expansion, or Even Adam Did Get Bored Eventually.

Tipcode EGTR-001

This Tipcode sounds the six guitar strings, from low E to high E.

String numbers
The six strings have numbers too. Confusingly, they're numbered the other way around, from high to low: The thin, high-sounding E-string is referred to as the *first string*. As a reminder: The thinnest string has the 'thinnest' number, the 1.

Wound strings
On most electric guitars, the three thickest strings are wound with metal wire. The extra mass of the metal winding helps these *wound strings* to sound as low as they should. The three thinnest strings (B and E) are *plain strings*.

Bass strings
The strings of a bass guitar have the same note names as the four

Tipcode EGTR-002

This Tipcode sounds the four strings of a bass guitar: E, A, D, and G.

lowest guitar strings: E, A, D, G, from thick to thin. They sound an octave lower than the guitar strings.

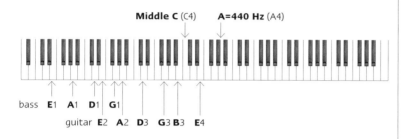

Middle C (C4)   **A=440 Hz** (A4)

bass   **E**1   **A**1   **D**1   **G**1

guitar   **E**2   **A**2   **D**3   **G**3 **B**3   **E**4

The four strings of an electric bass are tuned an octave lower than the four lowest guitar strings. A=440 (key A4) is the pitch most instruments are tuned to (see page 132).

Numbered octaves

To avoid confusion between higher and lower sounding notes of the same name, the notes and octaves have been numbered. The low E-string on a guitar is E2. High E is E4. If the guitar has twenty four-frets, the highest note you can play is E6.

Bass notes

Low E on a bass sounds one octave below the low E of a guitar, i.e., E1. This is the first E of the piano keyboard.

> ### Twice as thick
>
> To make the bass strings sound as low as they do, they're about twice as thick as the corresponding guitar strings, and a lot longer. All bass strings are wound strings.

TIP

HARDWARE

The metal parts of a guitar are collectively known as the *hardware*.

Tuning machines

The strings are tuned with the *tuning machines*, which are also known as *tuning gears, tuners, (tuning) pegs,* or *machine heads.*

11

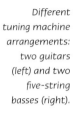

Different tuning machine arrangements: two guitars (left) and two five-string basses (right).

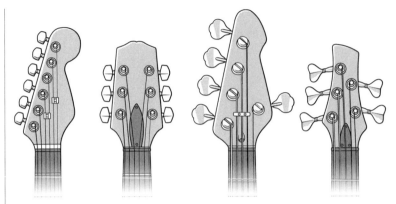

Nut
Between the head and the fingerboard, the strings run through the slots in the *nut*. These slots keep the strings properly spaced.

Bridge
From the nut, the strings run along the fingerboard, past the pickups, toward the *bridge*.

Saddles
At the bridge, each string runs over a *saddle*. These saddles or *bridge saddles* can be used to adjust the instrument. Most types of bridges have one saddle per string.

Tailpiece
The strings are attached either to the bridge or to a separate *stopbar tailpiece*.

TIPCODE

Tipcode EGTR-003
The tremolo can be used for pitch bend and vibrato effects, as this Tipcode shows.

12

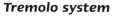

Tremolo system

Many guitars have a *tremolo system* or *trem*. Moving the trem arm makes all the strings go down — or up — in pitch simultaneously, which allows for pitch bend and vibrato effects.

PICKUPS AND CONTROLS

Most guitars have two or three pickups; most basses have one or two.

Bridge and neck pickups

If you play the strings close to the bridge, you'll get a brighter, edgier sound than if you play them close to the neck. Likewise, the pickup that's closest to the bridge produces a brighter, edgier sound than the *neck pickup* — even if they're exactly the same pickups.

Selector

On guitars, the *pickup selector* allows you to choose which pickup(s) you use, so you can vary your sound.

Balance

Basses often have a *balance control* that allows you to blend the sound of the bridge and neck pickups, or use just one of them.

Volume controls

Some instruments have two *volume controls*, rather than one. These controls can also be used to mix the sound of two pickups.

Tone

The *tone control(s)* can be used to make the sound a bit darker, warmer, or less bright.

Output jack

The signal produced by the pickups goes to the amp through a cable, which connects to the instrument's *output jack* or *output socket*.

13

More outputs

A growing number of instruments can be hooked up directly to your computer or other digital equipment. For that purpose, they come with an extra output. A USB socket, for example, allows you to connect the instrument directly to your computer (for recording or practicing purposes, for example), without the need for an external audio interface.

HOLLOW-BODY ELECTRICS

Compared to solidbodies, *hollow-body* electric guitars produce a warmer, mellower, or rounder sound. For a warmer, vintage type of sound, bassists often use a hollow-body bass guitar.

The top

While most acoustic guitars have a flat top, hollow-body electrics usually have an arched top, much like a violin. Another similarity with this bowed instrument is the *f*-shape of the soundholes. Electric guitars with an arched top are often referred to as *archtops*.

Floating bridge

Hollowbodies typically have a one-piece *floating bridge*, held in place only by the pressure of the strings. The tailpiece and pickguard are also floating designs.

Feedback

Hollow-body guitars and basses are very susceptible to *feedback*. This is the loud *skreee* you also hear if you accidentally point a microphone at a loudspeaker. To reduce feedback, most shallower models have a solid wooden block built into the soundbox. This block also improves the sustain of the instrument. Such guitars are often used by blues and fusion players.

Many different names

The many different names used for shallow hollow-body instruments, with or without a center block, are quite confusing.

14

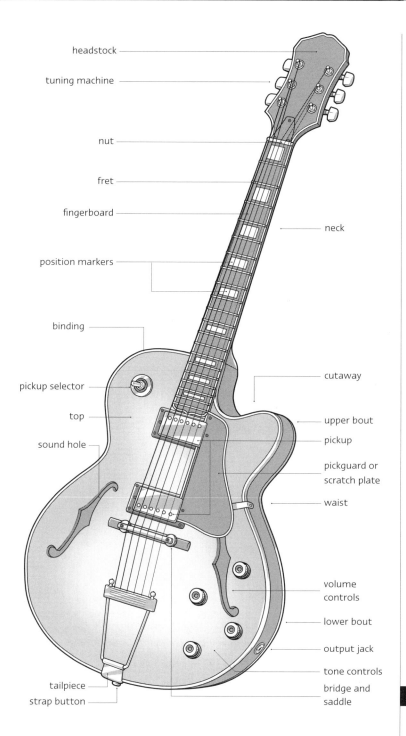

headstock

tuning machine

nut

fret

fingerboard

neck

position markers

binding

pickup selector

cutaway

top

upper bout

sound hole

pickup

pickguard or
scratch plate

waist

volume
controls

lower bout

output jack

tone controls

bridge and
saddle

tailpiece

strap button

15

They range from *semi-solid* to *semi-hollow*, and from *thinline* to *slimline* — and there are no set definitions.

LEFT-HANDED INSTRUMENTS

Right-handed bassists and guitarists play the strings with their right hand, and they fret them with their left. Many left-handed players do it the other way around, playing a 'left-handed' instrument, as shown below. As righties outnumber lefties by far, most shops carry just a limited number of left-handed guitars and basses. Some companies charge a higher price for them; others don't.

The other way around
On left-handed instruments, everything is 'the other way around.' If not, the trem arm and the controls would be in an awkward

A 'left-handed' solid-body.

TIP

Hendrix
Some lefties use regular instruments, most notably the late guitar great Jimi Hendrix. Others prefer a left-handed instrument with the strings in the 'right-handed' order. One example would be bassist Jimmy Haslip.

16

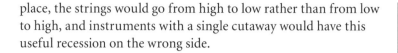

place, the strings would go from high to low rather than from low to high, and instruments with a single cutaway would have this useful recession on the wrong side.

AMPLIFIERS

Most guitarists and bass players use a *combo amplifier*: an amplifier and one or more speakers in one unit.

Character
An amplifier does a lot more than just boosting sound. It also lends a certain character or color to it: If you play your guitar through different amps, it'll sound different each time. And just as there are special guitars for certain styles of music, some types of amps are better suited for heavy metal, and others for jazz, for example.

Speakers
The speaker or speakers used with the amp play a major role in the sound too. After all, when you play amplified, the speaker is the part that makes the air vibrate, thus producing sound.

Two parts
The actual amplifier is made up of a *preamplifier* and a *power amp*. The preamp is used to manipulate the sound with volume, tone, and other controls. The power amp, as its name indicates, supplies the power.

Gain
In addition to one or more volume controls, most amplifiers have a *gain* control. On many guitar amps, you use this control to set the amount of distortion you want.

Two channels
Most modern guitar amps have two *channels*. You use the clean, normal, or rhythm channel for a clean, undistorted sound. Most

17

players use this channel when they play chords. The second channel is the one you use for a distorted solo or lead sound. It's known as the drive, overdrive, lead, or crunch channel.

Tipcode EGTR-004
This Tipcode briefly demonstrates the difference between a clean and a distorred sound.

Controls and footswitch
On most amps, each channel has its own volume control, and it's good to have separate tone controls for each channel too. Two-channel amps usually come with a footswitch that allows you to change channels from a distance.

Gain for basses
On bass amps, the gain control is not generally used to set the amount of distortion (most bassists use a clean sound), but to adjust the amp to the signal strength of the bass: Some basses have a much stronger signal than others.

Solid state or tubes
Amplifiers use either *transistors* (*solid state amplifiers*) or *tubes* for the actual amplification of the signal. Many players favor the more expensive tube amps for what's often described as a warmer, fatter type of sound. Besides these two basic types of amps, there are hybrid models, e.g., amplifiers with a tube preamp and a solid state power amp.

Power
A major factor when buying an amp is what *power rating* to go for. For home practicing purposes, a small 10- or 15-watt amp

18

> ## Modeling amps
>
> *Modeling amps use digital technology to emulate the sound of well-known amplifiers of various makes. This type of amp usually features a wide variety of digital effects too.*

TIP

will usually do. For performances in small venues you'll soon need some 50 to 100 watts. Bass amps usually have a higher power rating than the amp of the guitarist in the same band: Low frequencies require more energy and thus more watts to be properly amplified.

There's more

Contrary to general belief, the power rating of an amp doesn't tell you how loud it can sound per se; there are many more factors that

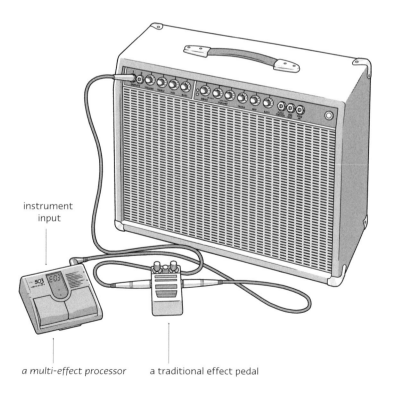

instrument
input

a multi-effect processor   *a traditional effect pedal*

A guitar amplifier, a programmable multi-effect processor, and a traditional effect pedal.

19

come into play. *Tipbook Amplifiers and Effects* (see page 246) tells you everything you need to know.

EFFECTS

Most guitarists and many bass players use one or more effects to 'color' their sound. Amplifiers often have one or two effects built in, and sometimes more than that. You can expand your possibilities by adding *effect pedals* or *multi-effect processors* to your gear.

Reverb
Reverb is one of the most common effects. It makes your sound bigger, adding lots of space to it. Most guitar amps come with a built-in reverb.

Distortion
As mentioned above, you can generate a distorted guitar sound by turning up the gain on your amplifier. Alternatively, you can use a separate distortion effect pedal. There are dozens of effect pedals available, producing a wild array of distortion effects — from a relatively mild overdrive to a high-gain distortion — and with more or less illustrative names, ranging from Metal and Smokin' to Grunge and Grilled Cheese.

Other effects
Here are some other popular effects:

- When used subtly, a **chorus** makes your (bass) guitar sound thicker, richer, creamier, wider, fatter, or bigger than it really is. Often used on fretless basses and for jazzy guitar chords, for example, but a chorus can also be used to warm up a distorted guitar.

- **Delay** is also known as echo: It makes a copy of the sound and repeats it once or a number of times, with the echoes gradually getting softer. A delay allows for a wide range of effects; you can double your sound, create a 'rockabilly' slapback sound, or use long delay times to create harmonies with the notes you just played.

- A **wah-wah** does exactly what its name suggests.

- Other effects include **flangers**, **phasers** (both related to chorus), **pitch shifters** (add extra notes to the notes you play), **fuzz boxes** (another type of distortion), **tremolos** (rapidly vary the volume level) **compressors** (popular among bass players, making for a tight sound) — and there's much more available.

Tipcode EGTR-005
This Tipcode demonstrates various popular effects such as a wah-wah, a chorus, and a delay.

TIPCODE

Effect pedals
The traditional effect pedals usually have a footswitch to turn the effect on and off, and three or more dedicated controls. On a delay pedal, for example, you can set the volume of the effect, how long you will hear the effect, how often the notes are repeated, and the delay time — from thousandths of a second to a second or more.

Multi effects
A multi-effect processor is a single unit that contains a number of effects, which can be either mixed or used individually. Most have a number of pedals and a programming section, so you can design your sounds at home and have them available onstage by the flick of a pedal. They often feature a built-in metronome (see page 29), a tuner (see page 129), and a headphone jack so you can use it for silent practice too. Effects and multi-effect processors or signal processors also come in rack-mountable and desktop formats.

21

Combined

Effect pedals and multi effects can be combined, of course. In the setup on page 19, the instrument cable is plugged into the multi-effect unit. The guitar signal is first processed by the multi effect, and then by the effect pedal. The pedal is connected to the amp's instrument input.

There's more

The above is but a very brief introduction to the fascinating world of effects. If you want to know more on what they can do, and on how to select and use them, please check out *Tipbook Amplifiers and Effects* (see page 246).

3

Learning to Play

Guitars and basses are among the easiest instruments to get started on. With just a little talent and practice you can get yourself to play some basic songs in just a few weeks. Learning to play these instruments really well and make them sound good takes a lot more time, of course, and you can easily spend a lifetime learning to really master them.

You can play numerous rock and pop songs on guitar as soon as you've mastered a few basic chords. Learning these chords is basically a matter of studying *chord diagrams:* charts that simply and clearly indicate where to put your fingers for each chord.

Play string 3 at the first fret with your index finger, play string 5 at the second fret with your middle finger, and play string 4 at the second fret with your ring finger. The result is an E-major chord.

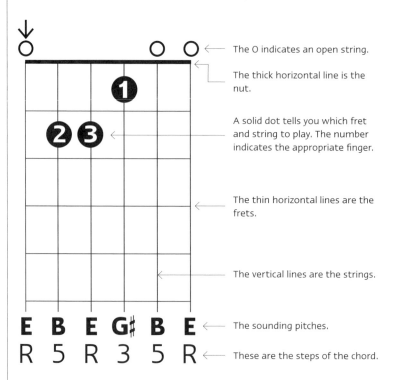

The O indicates an open string.

The thick horizontal line is the nut.

A solid dot tells you which fret and string to play. The number indicates the appropriate finger.

The thin horizontal lines are the frets.

The vertical lines are the strings.

The sounding pitches.

These are the steps of the chord.

Books and digital chord finders

Starting on page 197 of this book you'll find numerous chord diagrams. Similar charts are available online as well, and various companies make miniature digital chord finders that you can take along to rehearsals — some even featuring a built-in tuner, right-hand and left-hand modes, and a touch screen. These chord

Songbooks
Many songbooks come with chord diagrams for each song, allowing you to easily master your favorite hits.

finders or chord dictionaries easily house some 4,000 or more chords.

Tablature

Basically, chord charts are a shortcut for reading the notes of the chords in traditional notation. There's a similar solution for guitar solos and bass lines, called *tablature* or *tabs*. Horizontal lines represent the strings of your (bass) guitar, and numbers are used to indicate where to fret (or *stop*) the strings and which fingers to use. Many songbooks include tab notation. Tablature doesn't allow for precise rhythmical notation, so traditional notation may be included.

The numbers of the strings.

The tablature staff represents a guitar neck.

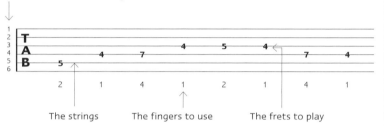

The strings   The fingers to use   The frets to play

Reading music

Chord diagrams and tablature offer an easy way to learn to play an instrument without having to read music in the traditional sense. Still, it's not a bad idea to learn how to read traditional notation too. Why?

- Traditional notation gives you access to **loads of books and magazines** with exercises, songs, and solos.

- It'll provide you with **better insight** into the way chords and songs are structured.

- It enables you to **put down on paper** your own songs, solos, ideas, and exercises — not just for (bass) guitarists, but for other musicians as well.

- It enables you to read parts that were not **written for guitarists or bassists**.

- It makes you **more of a musician**, instead of 'just' a (bass) guitarist.

25

- As it widens the range of gigs you can play, it **broadens your career options**.

- And finally: **It isn't that hard** at all. *Tipbook Music on Paper – Basic Theory* (see page 248) teaches you the basics within a few chapters.

LESSONS

Even while there are so many — successful — self-taught players, consulting a teacher isn't a bad idea either. Getting the basics down helps you to start out the right way, and if you find yourself stuck in your learning process later on, a good teacher will help you to get going again.

The right teacher
If you take a little bit of time, you'll be able to find a teacher who's willing and able to teach you the style of music you want to play, be it pop, jazz, or punk.

More than just how to play
Good teachers teach you more than just how to play chords and solos or bass lines. They'll teach you technique, how to produce a good tone, good posture, and practice and tuning routines, for example, and they can introduce you to different styles of music.

Questions, questions
On your first visit to a teacher, don't just ask how much it costs. Here are some other questions.

- Is an **introductory lesson** included? This is a good way to find out how well you get on with the teacher, and for that matter, with the instrument.

- Is the teacher interested in taking you on as a student even if you are doing it **just for the fun of it**, or will he or she expect you to practice at least three hours a day?

- Do you have to make a large investment in **method books** right away, or is the course material provided?

- Can you **record your lessons**, so that you can listen again to how you sounded and what was said when you get home?

- Will you be allowed to concentrate fully on the style of music you want to play, or will you be required — or inspired — to **learn other styles as well**?

Finding a teacher

Looking for a private teacher? Music stores may have teachers on their staff, or they may be able to refer you to one. You can also consult your local Musician's Union or the band director at a high school. Do check the classified ads in newspapers, in music magazines, or on supermarket bulletin boards. Teachers can also be found online (see page 195 for some starting points), and some players have found great teachers in musicians they have seen in performance.

Prices

Professional private teachers will usually charge between twenty-five and seventy-five dollars per hour. Some make house calls, for which you'll pay extra.

Group or individual lessons

Instead of taking individual lessons, you can go for group lessons, if that's an option in your vicinity. Private lessons are more expensive, but can be tailored exactly to your needs.

Collectives

You may want to check whether there are any teacher collectives or music schools in your vicinity. These collectives usually offer extras such as playing in bands, master classes, and clinics, in a wide variety of styles and at various levels.

Acoustic lessons

Many electric players studied the acoustic guitar as well, and your 'electric sound' may benefit from 'acoustic lessons.' How come? For one thing, because it takes more effort to make an acoustic

27

instrument sound really good — so being able to make an acoustic guitar sound good can easily improve your tone on an electric one.

PRACTICING

You can learn to play without reading notes, and even without a teacher. But you can't do without practicing.

How long?

How long you need to practice depends on what you want to achieve. Many great instrumentalists have practiced four to eight hours a day for years, or more. The more time you spend practicing (and playing!), the faster you improve. Half an hour a day usually results in steady progress.

Shorter sessions

If you find it hard to practice half an hour a day, try dividing it up into two quarter-hour sessions, or three of ten minutes each.

TIP

Setting goals

Rather than focusing on how long you need to practice, it may be wise to set a goal for each practice session, or for the next week. That allows you to concentrate on the music, rather than on the clock!

Books, videos, and more

Guitarists and bassists have easy access to tons of practice and reading material:

- There are **bass and guitar** books for absolute beginners and absolute pros. Quite a few of them have a tape or CD with examples or play-along exercises; you turn off the sound of the (bass) guitarist and play that part yourself.

28

- **Guitar and bass magazines** typically include lessons, charts, tabs, and other educational stuff.

- **Instructional videos** can be very helpful. They're available for many styles and all levels.

- There's **software** that turns your computer into a guitar or bass teacher.

- The **Internet** can help you improve your playing too: online lessons are available at various websites (see page 194).

Keeping time

Most songs are supposed to be played at a steady tempo. Practicing with a *metronome* helps you to do so, developing your inner sense of time. A metronome is a small mechanical or electronic device that ticks or beeps out a steady, adjustable pulse, which helps you to work on your tempo, timing, and rhythm.

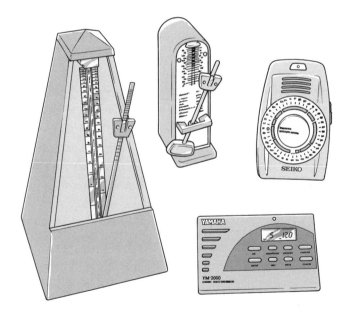

Two mechanical metronomes and two electronic ones.

Drum machines and more

A drum machine is a great alternative to the metronome. There are similar machines that can play programmable bass lines or

29

guitar chords too, and some can sound like a full band that you can play along with.

Phrase trainers

Phrase trainers are devices that can slow down a musical phrase from a CD of an MP3 file, for example, so you can figure out even the meanest, fastest licks at your own tempo. These machines may also feature an integrated guitar preamp, a tuner, a metronome, and a series of digital effects. Some also offer a range of virtual (bass) guitar amplifiers that you can choose from.

TIP

Record your music

No matter how good you are, it's always hard to judge your own playing as you play. Tip: record your practice session, or your first or subsequent attempts to play the piece that you have been practicing, and then judge your performance by listening to the recording, once or a couple of times. This is very instructive for musicians at any level. Also consider recording your lessons, so you can listen once more to what was said, and especially how you sounded, when you get home. All you need is a portable recording device with a built-in microphone — although better equipment yields better and more enjoyable results.

A computer is great for recording too; you can hook your guitar up to it using an (USB) audio interface. Ask your dealer for more information. Tip: Some instruments feature a USB output for recording and other purposes (see page 95).

No noise

One of the great things about electric guitars and basses is that you can practice for hours without bothering anyone. First of all, there are plenty of things you can practice without using an amplifier at all, ranging from your technique to scales and chords. If you want to hear your true 'electric' sound when practicing, you can use a special pocket-sized practice amp, an even smaller headphone amp that you simply plug into your guitar output, or any (bass) guitar amp that comes with a headphone jack. Most multi-effect units have a headphone output for silent practicing as well, and you can even connect your instrument to your computer (see page 14) and use your computer head phones. Warning: If you use headphones, keep the volume down to prevent hearing damage.

Hearing damage

Most bands play and practice at volumes that can cause hearing loss or hearing damage pretty easily, so do consider using some kind of hearing protection, both at rehearsals and at gigs. As hearing loss is usually noticed only when it's too late (and it's typically irreversible), prevention is the key. Really.

Cheap or expensive earplugs...

The cheapest foam plastic earplugs, available from most music stores and drugstores, will make your band sound as if it's playing next door. The most expensive earplugs are custom-made to fit your ears. These plugs often have adjustable filters that reduce the volume without affecting the sound.

... and in between

Plastic earplugs come in many variations. Some just reduce the overall volume; others make the band sound dull and far away, just like earmuffs do. Also, some are easier to clean than others. Ask fellow musicians (drummers!) for their experiences with hearing protection, and don't hesitate to try different products until you find the ones that really fit and work for you. A hearing

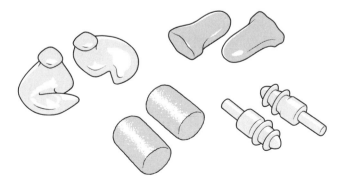

Some affordable types of ear plugs.

31

aid will cost more in the long run, and ringing ears (*tinnitus*) never stop ringing.

Get to work

Finally, visit as many concerts as you can. One of the best ways to learn to play is seeing other musicians at work. Living legends or local amateurs — every gig's a learning experience. And the very best way to learn to play? Play a lot!

4

Buying a (Bass) Guitar

You can get a brand new electric guitar and an amp for a couple of hundred dollars, and you can just as easily spend thousands. The same goes for basses and bass amps. This chapter tells you the basics on instrument prices, music stores, buying new or secondhand, and more. Chapters 5, 6, and 8 deal with what to pay attention to once you're in a store.

Some hundred fifty to two hundred dollars is all you need to get yourself a brand new solid-body electric, and a decent practice amp should cost about the same.

Starter packs

Many stores offer complete sets that include everything you need to start playing: the instrument, a small amplifier, a cable, a pick, an electronic tuner, a gig bag, and perhaps a guitar stand as well. These so-called *starter packs* or *gig rigs* start at less than three hundred dollars.

... for a couple of hundred dollars...

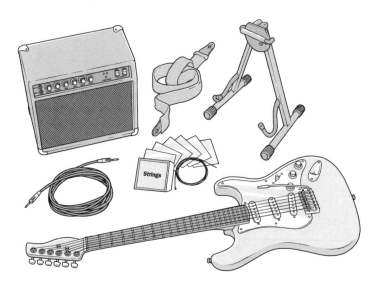

The very cheapest

Teachers often advise against buying the very cheapest instruments. As with any other type of product, you can't expect a lot of quality for little money. Still, you can have years of musical fun with a budget (bass) guitar.

Hard to spot

It can be hard to spot the differences between budget, midrange, and expensive basses and guitars, especially for beginning players. Most affordable instruments look as if they should cost a lot more than they do — and some also sound much better than their price suggests!

34

Amps and effects

If you're going to play gigs and need to bring your own amp, be prepared to spend a minimum of some three or four hundred dollars. Bass guitars need more power, so bassists often need to spend a little more. Most guitarists and many bassists also use one or more effects. Effect pedals start around thirty dollars. The most affordable multi-effect processors are available for around three to four times that price. Top-of-the-line models may cost well over a thousand dollars.

Four or more

A solid-body instrument that sounds, tunes, and plays well enough to be used on gigs can be yours for as little as three to four hundred dollars. Hollow-body guitars are more expensive than solidbodies of similar quality.

Better quality

Spending more on a guitar buys you better wood, hardware, pickups, workmanship, and quality control, to mention some of the main points. Their combined result is an instrument that can be expected to sound better, play better, and feel better, to last longer, and to have a higher resale value — and you may just enjoy it a lot more than a cheap one too. Usually, more money also buys you more options: more finishes to choose from, various pickup configurations, and so on.

Custom-made

If you want to have even more options, you can have an instrument custom-made. Several guitar brands have custom shops, and there are many individual guitar makers and guitar and bass workshops around. Hand-made instruments usually start around two to three thousand dollars, and go up to ten times that price, and more.

Adjustments

No matter how good an instrument is, it'll never play well and sound good until it has been properly tuned and adjusted.

35

Unfortunately, this is not always the case with the instruments on display in music stores — especially when it comes to the lower budget guitars and basses. An experienced player can help you tell the badly adjusted instruments from the ones you really shouldn't buy.

THE STORE

The more instruments a store has on display, the harder it is to choose. On the other hand, as selecting (bass) guitars is largely a matter of comparing them, a wide selection is exactly what you need. It's equally important to meet salespeople who enjoy their work and know what they're talking about. One more tip? Visit several music stores, and talk to various salespeople, as they all have their own 'sound' too.

Time
Take your time when buying an instrument. You'll probably have to live with it for years. On the other hand, many players ended up buying that one guitar they liked straightaway, after just the first few notes.

Take someone along
If you just started playing, it'll be hard if not impossible to judge an instrument. The best advice is to take a more experienced player along when you go shopping, or select stores where they have musicians on staff.

Buying online
You can also buy your guitar online or by mail order. This makes it impossible to compare instruments, of course, but most online and mail-order companies offer a return service for most or all of their products: If you're not happy with the instrument you ordered, you can return it within a certain period of time. Of course the instrument should be in new condition when you send it back.

SECONDHAND

If you don't want to spend too much, but you don't want to play the cheapest instrument either, you may consider buying secondhand. Used instruments by well-known brands often sell for more than equally good ones from lesser-known makers. You may want to take that into account when you buy a new one too.

Privately or in a store?

Purchasing a used instrument from a private party may be cheaper than buying the same one from a store. One of the advantages of buying a used guitar in a store, though, is that you can go back if you have questions. Also, some music stores may offer you a limited warranty on your purchase. Another difference is that a good dealer won't usually ask an outrageous price, but a private seller might, either because he doesn't know any better, or because he thinks that you don't.

TIP

Vintage guitars

Many players favor older instruments, made in the 1960s, the 1950s, or before, because of their tone, their looks, or their history, because they're rare, or all of the above. Such vintage instruments can easily fetch a higher price than a new one of similar quality. Various guitar makers even market brand new 'old' instruments (relics; see page 41)!

MORE, MORE

If you want to know all there is to know, stock up on guitarists' and bassists' magazines that offer reviews of the latest gear. There is a lot of information available online, but be careful in selecting your sources and don't confuse opinions with facts. Some

37

informative websites are listed on page 194, and a number of (bass) guitar books can be found in that same section. *Tip:* Most (bass) guitar manufacturers have informative websites too, and the same goes for string makers, for example.

5

A Good Instrument

Guitars and basses come in numerous designs, sporting different shapes and sounds, dimensions, wood types, pickup configurations, necks, frets, strings, and so on. The knowledge presented in the following chapter will help you to make a choice, covering pretty much everything there is to look at and to listen for.

How a (bass) guitar sounds depends not only on the instrument itself and on the person who plays it, but also on the strings, the picks, the cables you're using, and of course on your amp and effects. Strings, picks, and cables are explored in Chapters 6 and 7 respectively. Amplifiers and effects are covered in a Tipbook by that title (see page 246).

This chapter
After exploring the various types of guitar finishes and bodies, this chapter covers the neck and fingerboard (page 47), the scale (string length; page 56), frets (58), tuning machines (61), the bridge (64), tremolos (67), pickups (72), tips on auditioning instruments (90), and much more.

Many variations
Few instruments come in as many designs as electric guitars and basses. Some are extremely versatile, created to be used in a wide variety of musical styles. Others are built for a specific type of music. Often their looks alone will tell: A heavy metal guitar looks very different from one that was designed for country music.

Surf on metal
Though you can play surf music on a guitar that was built for aggressive rock, it's usually better to use instruments for the style of music the designer had in mind. Likewise, knowing which guitar your favorite musician is playing can be a useful guide in finding the instrument that suits you best.

A sunburst finish.

40

Differing opinions

Musicians rarely agree about anything. The following chapters won't tell you who is right, or what is best, but rather how different experts think about different issues. You'll discover whom you agree with only by playing, and by listening to guitars or basses, and to the people who play them.

THE LOOKS

Guitar bodies can be finished with a single solid color; a natural, transparent lacquer; a two- or three-color sunburst finish; or with many other types and styles of finishes. Some companies even allow you to print your own photo or design on your instrument.

Plastic or natural

Most instruments have a polyurethane finish. This is a hard and durable synthetic type of lacquer. Natural finishes, such as nitrocellulose or oil, are typically used on more expensive

TIP

Relics

Vintage guitars and basses are so popular that some companies even offer brand-new 'vintage' instruments — artificially aged, with intentionally rusted hardware, discolored plastic parts, and skillfully damaged finishes. These instruments are generally referred to as relics. Some companies also offer vintage guitars that look as if they've been in someone's attic for several decades, with hairline cracks and a yellowed pickguard.

A replica is a copy of a (bass) guitar of another brand, and a reissue is a new edition of a older instrument, made by the original company.

41

instruments. These organic finishes, which tend to get darker with age, help bring out the instrument's resonance.

Pickguard
Pickguards come in lots of different colors and designs too. Laminated pickguards that show their three white-black-white plies at the edge are very popular. Most of today's pickguards are plastic. Unlike the traditional pickguard material (i.e., celluloid) they don't warp or expand.

Hardware
The hardware is usually black, shiny or matte chrome-plated, or gold-plated. On most instruments, the pickups or pickup covers perfectly match the hardware.

SOLIDBODIES

The type of wood used for the body affects both the instrument's tone and weight. The body shape influences the looks, the balance, and the playability of the instrument.

Chipboard or solid wood
The very cheapest guitars often have a chipboard or plywood body. A body that consists of one or more pieces of solid wood helps produce more sustain and a richer sound.

Different wood, different sound
Generally speaking, denser types of wood promote a brighter tone and more sustain than lighter types of wood. That said, many types of wood come in different variations and qualities. Also, the way a guitar is built can completely alter some the wood's typical characteristics, and experts don't always agree when it comes to describing the effect of certain types of wood. The message? Always listen to the instrument as a whole, rather than focusing on the type of wood it's made of. Still, it's good to have some basic knowledge of the subject.

Light or heavy

Poplar, basswood, and alder are three lighter types of wood. They're often said to help produce a warmer, fuller, fatter type of sound. Maple, at the other end of the spectrum, is very dense, and thus makes for a brighter tone.

Weights and densities

Mahogany and ash come in various weights and densities. The lighter types, again, enhance a warmer, mellower tone. Denser wood promotes a brighter, 'airier,' more open type of sound. Swamp ash is one of the lighter types of ash.

The top

Because of its beautiful appearance, maple is often used as top wood. It's available in many variations (i.e., quilted maple, bird's eye maple, and flamed or figured maple).

Choices

There are companies that offer a selection of ten, fifteen, or even more types of wood. When it comes to such choices, looks often play a larger role than sound. Likewise, with some instruments the wood you get depends on the finish you want.

Photo finish

On some instruments, the 'wooden' top is not real flame wood, but a thin photographic film that is applied to the body. It often takes an expert eye to distinguish such a 'photo flame' from the real thing, which typically has more depth and character (in sound too!).

Synthetic bodies

Bodies can also be made entirely of synthetics, or carbon fiber, for example. Some players praise their consistency; others miss the depth and warmth caused by the natural inconsistencies of wood.

TIP

Thick

The size and shape of the body influence sound, weight, and

43

playing comfort. Generally speaking, a thicker, heavier body increases the sustain and makes for a richer sound.

Weight

A 'heavy' solid-body can outweigh a light one by three or four pounds. This doesn't sound like much, but you may very well feel the difference after a couple of songs.

Balance

The balance of the instrument is just as important. A neck-heavy guitar can be more tiresome to play than one that actually weighs more, but has a better balance. An uncomfortable balance can sometimes be cured, for example by relocating the strap buttons. A tip: If you usually play standing up, audition instruments standing up as well.

Solid?

Solidbodies aren't completely solid. True solid-body guitars have at least some cavities for the pickups, the wiring, and the pots, for example.

Solid guitar body with cavities for the pickups and controls.

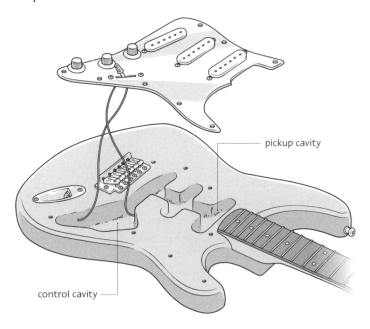

pickup cavity

control cavity

Sound chambers

Other instruments also have one or more invisible *sound chambers* that reduce the weight and make for a warmer tone. Their names (*chambered* bodies or *semi-hollow* bodies) are also used for shallow-body guitars that clearly show their sound chamber through a soundhole in the top.

Contoured bodies

Today, most instruments have contoured bodies with rounded edges. These designs don't dig in your chest the way some old-style, non-contoured *slab* bodies do.

The heel

The accessibility of the highest frets depends on the depth of the cutaway, but also on the *heel*, where the neck meets the body. The less pronounced the heel is, the less it'll be in your way when reaching for the highest notes. A thicker heel, on the other hand, is said to make for a more solid, full-bodied sound — just like a heavier body or a thicker neck.

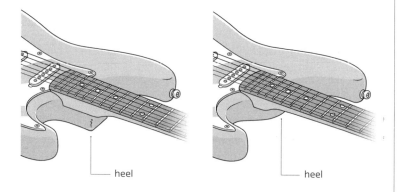

heel   heel

The right-hand design allows for easier access to the highest frets.

HOLLOWBODIES

Hollow-body instruments come with shallow and deep bodies, with one or two cutaways, with or without a center block, and in various types of wood.

45

Jazz

Traditionally, jazz players favor a big-box guitar or jazz box. These instruments are often 17" wide at the lower bout, and about 3.5" to 4.5" deep. (This dimension is known as the *rim thickness*).

The rim thickness of a jazz guitar.

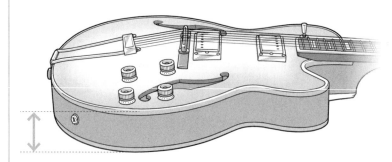

Shallow with block

The deeper the body is, the more sensitive it is to feedback. This explains why guitarists in loud bands usually opt for shallower models. These guitars often come with a built-in center block that reduces feedback even more, besides enhancing the instrument's sustain. Most hollow-body basses have a similar center block. Some instruments leave a little space between this *sustain block* and the top, promoting the acoustic qualities of the instrument.

Semi-solid, semi-acoustic

Instruments with a center block are often referred to as semisolids, while the ones without a block are indicated as semi-acoustic instruments — but the same terms are used for different types of instruments as well.

Hollow-body top

The top is one of the most fundamental parts of a hollow-body (bass) guitar. A solid spruce top is usually said to provide the warmest, deepest, most acoustic type of sound. A maple top makes for a brighter tone. Laminated and pressed arched tops tend to produce a shallower and less dynamic sound than tops that are carved from a solid piece of wood. Solid tops are usually *bookmatched* (see page 174).

46

Cutaway

A cutaway with a pointed 'horn' is known as a Florentine cutaway. A Venetian cutaway has a rounded shape. The same terms are used for acoustic guitars, shown below.

Florentine and Venetian cutaways, shown on acoustic steel-string guitars.

NECK AND FINGERBOARD

The neck and fingerboard affect both the playability and the sound of the instrument. As with the body, heavier and denser types of wood promote a brighter, richer, more solid sound and sustain. Using more wood (i.e., having a thicker, wider neck) has roughly the same effect.

Thin or thick

'Fast' players often prefer relatively thin necks, as do musicians

47

with small hands. Thicker necks not only feel differently, but also enhance the instrument's stability and tone. Rolled, rounded, or beveled edges can make for a more comfortable, broken-in feel.

V, D, C, U

Neck back profiles are often indicated with a letter that resembles their shape. However, the letters used do not always refer to the same types of neck. For example, some players use the letter C for a rounded, smooth 1960s profile; others use the same letter for thin, low-profile necks. Likewise, some think C and D are similar, while others use D for mid-1980s, square-edge neck designs. V-type necks have a clearly distinguishable 'ridge', and U-necks are typically very thick.

Different neck thicknesses and profiles, different fingerboards...

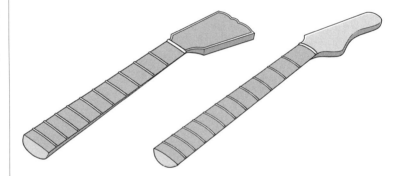

Asymmetrical

Asymmetrical necks are rare, but some five- and six-string bass necks are a little fatter under the low B-string.

Width

The neck width is usually measured at the nut. The wider it is, the further apart the strings will be. For fast solos, most players prefer a tighter string spacing. Conversely, clean chords are easier on a wider neck. Slapping bass players usually prefer a wider string spacing than finger-style players, who pluck the strings. Neck widths range from about 1.57" to 1.75" (40–45 mm) on guitars. Bass necks start around 1.5". On some basses, string spacing can be adjusted at the bridge (see page 65).

48

More strings

Instruments with extra strings (seven-string guitars; basses with five or more strings) usually have wider necks too. For example, most five-string bass necks are between 1.75" and 1.80" at the nut.

TIP

Wider neck

Extra strings extend your tonal range, and the extra neck wood is said to make for a slightly rounder sound with added mids — but you do need to get used to playing such an instrument, because of both the wider neck and the extra strings. Also, certain playing techniques will always be easier on an instrument with the traditional number of strings.

More strings, more money

Many basses are available in four-, five-, and six-string models. In the lower and intermediate price ranges, an 'extra string' typically costs fifty to a hundred dollars more.

Wide necks:
a seven-string
bass
(Groove Tools).

Radius

If you look along the neck of a (bass) guitar, you'll see that the fingerboard is curved, rising slightly toward the middle strings. The exact curvature is indicated by the _radius_.

49

More inches, flatter fingerboard

The radius is usually given in inches. The higher the figure, the flatter the fingerboard. A 7.25" radius indicates a strongly curved fingerboard; a fingerboard with a 14" radius is pretty flat. Most of today's guitars have fingerboards that range from 9.5" (e.g., Fender) to 14" (modern rock guitars), with 10" (e.g., PRS) and 12" radiuses (e.g., Gibson) as in-between examples.

Your radius

What's best for you may depend as much on your playing style as on personal preference. Many players find a highly curved fingerboard very comfortable, especially when playing chords. A flat fingerboard, on the other hand, allows for high-note string bends without choking the strings to the frets higher up the neck. Generally speaking, a radius from 9.5" to 11" or 12" will work for most playing styles and styles of music.

The radius tells you how flat or rounded the fingerboard is (actual dimensions shown).

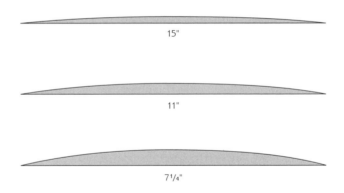

15"

11"

7¹/₄"

Compound radius

A *compound radius* fingerboard becomes flatter toward the body. It may change from from 10" at the nut (for comfortable chord fingering) to 14" or 16" at the body (for choke-free high-register string bends), for example.

Wood

Maple and mahogany are commonly used materials for guitar necks. Maple necks typically make for a brighter, more transparent

50

type of sound. Mahogany tends to enhance a warmer tone with a stronger midrange. It's hard to judge the quality of a neck, but it should have a straight, even grain along its entire length. Necks can be made of one solid block, or built up of several pieces (and types) of wood.

Fingerboard

Rosewood and maple are the two most commonly used woods for the fingerboard. Rosewood fingerboards, with a dark brown hue, help produce a warm sound with an accented midrange, typically loved by rock players. Maple fingerboards are often one with the neck, rather than being a separate, glued-on piece of wood. They're blonde and lacquered, and make for a brighter, punchier tone with more bite and attack.

Ebony, a nearly black, extremely hard type of wood, is used mainly on expensive basses. Some consider it too brittle to properly hold the frets; softer, 'springier' types of wood (such as maple and rosewood) have a tighter grip on the frets.

Bright or warm?

Of course, the type of wood used for the fingerboard is just one of the many elements that make for the sound of an instrument. This helps explain why some describe the effect of a pau ferro fingerboard as bright, while others define it as warm.

Composite

A few brands use either composite (phenol) fingerboards, which have a very smooth, 'plastic' feel, or phenolic-impregnated wooden fingerboards. The latter, also known as Pheno-wood fingerboards, are harder and more durable than pure wood, and they have a more natural feel and a better tone than phenol.

Dots, stars, stripes...

Usually, the position markers or *fingerboard markers* are simple dot inlays. There are plenty of other shapes available though, ranging from stars and blocks to bow ties, dice, and thunderbolts. No matter what they're made of (e.g., abalone, shell, or mother-of-pearl; pearloid; other materials), they do not affect the sound of the instrument.

51

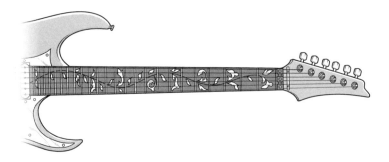

Set-in or bolt-on?

Necks can be glued or bolted onto the body. Most players find that instruments with *bolt-on necks* sound brighter and punchier, with a faster, stronger and more percussive attack, and with less sustain than the ones with glued *set* or *set-in necks*. However, some of these differences can also be due to the thicker type of body that most instruments with set-in necks have, among other things.

Through-neck

A *through-neck* is a neck that runs all the way from the headstock to the tail of the instrument. This *neck-through body* or *full-length neck* design is said to enhance the instrument's sustain. It's more commonly found on basses than on guitars.

52

Truss rod slot

On instruments with a one-piece neck and fingerboard, the adjustable truss rod is inserted from the back. A dark strip of wood, visible at the back of the neck, covers the slot.

From the side

Most truss rods have their adjustment nut either at the headstock (hidden under a small cover), or at the other end of the neck. In the latter case, you may have to remove the pickguard to get to it. Also, there are truss rods that can be conveniently adjusted from the side of the neck. A warning: Neck adjustments are best left to a guitar technician.

Dual action

Typically, the truss rod is used to prevent the neck from getting too concave as a result of the strings' tension. A *dual-action* or *two-way* truss rod also allows the neck to be adjusted the other way around, making it a bit more concave than it was. Installing higher-tension (heavier-gauge) strings may have a similar effect — but you shouldn't change to different strings for this purpose, of course.

Graphite rods, carbon fiber spines

Some bass guitars and thin-neck guitars have rigid carbon fiber (graphite) rods to reinforce the neck, next to a truss rod. Other neck designs have a stiff, graphite core surrounded by feel- and sound-enhancing wood; the truss rod is located in a slot in this core.

TIP

One or both

There are two basic headstock designs. One has all tuning machines in line on one side (*6-in-line*). The other positions them on both sides of the headstock (*3L/3R*).

In line

With the tuning machines in line, the thin (treble) strings have to travel quite a few inches between the nut and their tuning machines. This can cause tuning instability when bending these strings or using a tremolo, unless your instrument has either an ultra smooth nut or a *locking nut* (see page 69). Also, the extra string length requires a slightly higher string tension. This makes the string harder to bend and more prone to breakage.

Reverse headstock

If this bothers you, consider trying a neck with a *reverse headstock*. This makes the instrument look like a right-handed guitar with a left-handed neck. As a result of reversing the headstock, the string section between the nut and the tuning machines is reduced for the treble strings (making them easier to bend and less susceptible to detuning), and increased for the bass strings (making them sound a bit tighter).

Tilted headstock

Many guitar and bass designs feature a *tilted headstock*, i.e., a headstock that is tilted slightly backward, usually at an angle of about 14°. This makes for a downward string tension at the nut, so that the strings don't pop out or buzz. Other designs require *string trees* or *string guides* for this purpose, as shown in the illustration below.

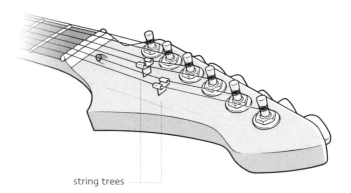

string trees

Sound, sustain, tuning stability

Do note that these small metal string guides may compromise your sound, sustain, and tuning stability (see page 69). As an alternative, you can use staggered tuning machines (see page 63).

Check the neck

If the neck and fingerboard don't feel as smooth as they should, on a new instrument, they need to be broken in. Always check to see if the neck is straight: It shouldn't bend to the left or the right, or be warped or twisted.

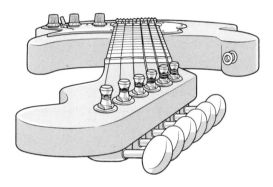

From this angle you can check whether a neck is warped or twisted.

Close to the edge

Also check whether the strings are spaced evenly across the neck. The illustration below shows a guitar with a slightly dislocated bridge. As a result, low E is so close to the edge that you keep pushing it off of the neck when playing the higher frets.

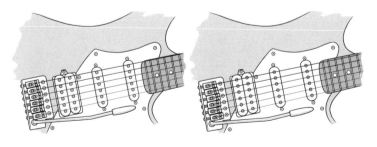

badly-placed bridge   well-placed bridge

On the guitar on the left, the low E-string is too close to the edge of the neck.

Dead spots

The fingerboard must be smooth and free from knots, cracks, and chips. Play each string in all positions, listening carefully for *dead spots.* These are positions where the tone suddenly drops off or sounds much softer. Do so both amplified and acoustically. However, some players are convinced that dead spots — to a certain extent — are pretty much unavoidable in great sounding instruments, stating that instruments without them usually sound consistently shallow and have little 'character.'

THE SCALE

Both guitars and basses come with different string lengths, known as the *scale.*

Range
Instruments with a longer scale tend to sound slightly fuller or warmer, with a bit of extra sustain, while instruments with shorter strings allow for easier fingering and faster licks. (Shorter strings are less tight than longer strings at the same pitch!) Also, on long-scale necks strings need to be bent further to get the required pitch.

Guitar scales
Most guitar scales are between 24" and 25.5" (62–65 cm). If you like much-lower-than-standard tunings, an instrument with an extra-long scale will help prevent buzzing strings (see page 165).

TIP

Smaller guitars
To enable young beginners to play the instrument, some companies make ³/₄ guitars, with scales that are about three to four inches shorter. Some players use these down-sized models as travel guitars. As an alternative, there's a guitar that folds in the middle, where neck and body meet. This 'Centerfold' takes up very little space when traveling.

56

Basses

Basses have much longer scales than guitars, ranging from 30" to 36". Most bassists go for a *long-scale* model (34"). Some players, including pros, prefer a *medium scale*, which is more comfortable to play, especially if you have smaller hands. *Short-scale* basses (30") are mainly used by children. Compared to the larger sizes, they tend to sound mellow, lacking a punchy low-end.

Extra-long

Super-long or extra-long scales (35"–36") are mainly used for five- and six-string basses, which have an extra low B-string. The extra length results in a higher string tension, which enhances the definition of low B as well as the instrument's overall focus and sustain. However, super-long scales do require large hands and flexible fingers. Also, the extra tension can make the G-string sound a bit nasal.

Speaking length

The scale is known also as the *vibrating length* or *speaking length* of the strings. However, the string sections between the nut and the tuning machines also vibrate, so they do influence the sound as well (see Reverse headstock, page 54, and String changes, page 70).

Measuring the scale

The correct way to determine the scale of an instrument is to double the distance from the nut to the center of the twelfth fret. Measuring from the nut to the saddles isn't very exact, as the saddles may be in a different position per string.

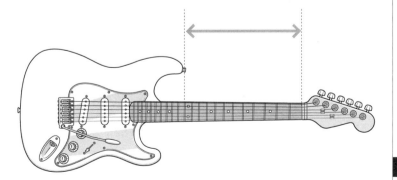

The scale: Double the distance from the nut to the twelfth fret.

FRETS

Most solidbodies have 21, 22, or 24 frets. The more frets, the larger your pitch range, of course. Still, many guitarists prefer instruments with 21 or 22 frets. Why? Because this design allows placement of the neck pickup exactly on the second-octave spot. On a 24-fret guitar, that's where the 24th fret is. Having 24 frets means that the neck pickup needs be positioned closer to the bridge, altering the sound it generates.

Basses
The number of frets on basses ranges from 20 on most traditional designs, to 24 or even 26 on other instruments.

Frets and sound
Frets come in different sizes and shapes. String bends are easiest on large, jumbo-type frets, seen usually on the type of guitars that are built for high-speed solos and lots of volume: 24 frets, a shallow neck, a flat fingerboard, a Floyd Rose-type tremolo, and humbuckers (see page 74) in the bridge and neck positions. Conversely, smaller (vintage) frets make chord playing and shifting up and down the neck easier. (Fretless bassists sometimes refer to frets as speed bumps.)

Shape
The shape of the frets has a minor impact on the sound. Broader designs tend to make for a slightly broader tone, while edgier frets promote a slightly edgier sound.

TIP

Zero fret
Some guitars and basses have a zero fret, right next to the nut. As a result, all strings always run over a fret — whether fretted or not — so open strings have the same timbre as fretted strings.

58

Check
Always check to see that there are no frets sticking out of the neck (making playing painful), and make sure the frets are long enough to prevent your E-strings from slipping off of the neck. Also, the frets should be leveled to prevent strings from buzzing of choking against them, and they should be properly rounded and polished to make for a smooth feel and easy string bends. Badly fitted or poorly finished frets can cause dead spots and buzzes – and so can worn frets.

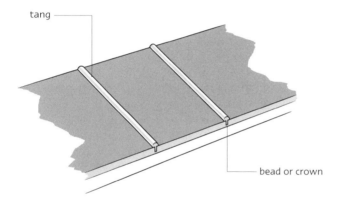

tang

bead or crown

Frets come in different sizes and shapes.

Nickel silver
Most frets are made of nickel silver, a hard type of alloy (containing no silver, incidentally…). However, fretting will eventually cause small dents in the frets that catch the strings and hinder string bending, and frequent bending will result in flat spots. Worn frets can be leveled, recrowned and sanded a couple of times by your guitar tech, until it's time to replace them.

Fretless basses and guitars
Many bassists prefer the sound of a *fretless bass*. Eliminating the metal frets gives these instruments a hard-to-describe, mellow, singing tone, a less percussive attack, and a characteristic sustain. It also makes playing in tune quite a bit harder: On a fretless instrument, the exact pitch of a note isn't determined by a fret, but by where exactly you put your finger on the fingerboard. Even the smallest deviation makes you sound out of tune. Fretless guitars are very rare, but they do exist.

59

TIPCODE

Tipcode EGTR-006
Listen to the difference between a
fretted and a fretless bass in this
Tipcode.

Stripes

To help you play in tune, some fretless basses have thin, inlaid
stripes instead of frets, showing you where to put your fingers. As
an alternative, fretless basses come with position markers on the
upper side of the neck.

*A fretless
bass guitar.*

Take them out

Rather then buying a fretless instrument, you can have the frets of
a fretted bass removed. The main disadvantage of this procedure

is that you can't tell what the bass will sound like in advance. You can have it refretted again if you don't like the result, of course, but buying a fretless instrument is much easier. The late Jaco Pastorius, probably the most famous fretless bassist ever, played on an instrument of which he had removed the frets, filling the resulting grooves with wood filler.

Different frets

If your guitar sounds perfectly in tune with some chords, one or two strings may be slightly off tune when you play another chord. This can be cured by applying special types of frets (see page 140), or by using a different tuning method (see page 138).

TUNING MACHINES

Good tuning machines are mainly important for precise, easy, and stable tuning, but there's more to them than just that.

Covered gears

Almost all guitars have enclosed tuning machines with sealed metal housings. Such *covered gear tuners* don't need additional lubrication. Non-sealed housings usually have a small opening that you can use to apply oil.

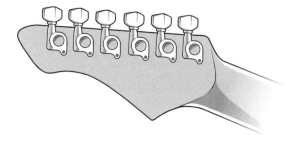

Sealed tuning machines; the standard on guitars.

Open tuners

Open tuning machines, where you can see the gears, are used on various bass guitar models and some types of vintage guitars.

These *open gear tuners* are more susceptible to dust and dirt, which is no problem as long as you keep them clean and (sparsely) lubricated. Applying a drop of light machine oil every half year will do for most open gear tuners.

Many basses have open tuning machines.

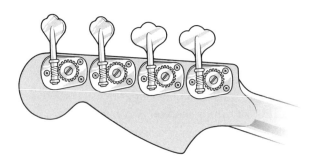

Adjustable tension
On some types of tuning machines the tension can be adjusted with the small screw on top of the button. Turning the screw makes the machine go tighter or looser.

Slotted machines
Most basses and some guitars have *slotted* or *split-shaft* tuning machines, with the hole for the string running lengthwise through the tuning post (or *shaft*). This cleans up the look as the string ends are hidden in the tuning posts. Also, slotted shaft tuners make fitting strings easier. On the other hand, they require that the strings be cut to length before they are fit. This can be

TIP

Finer control
The gear ratio of a tuning machine indicates how many times you need to turn the button to make the tuning post go round once. The higher the gear ratio, the finer the control it provides. Guitar tuning machines can be 12:1 or 14:1, but 16:1 or 18:1 is generally recommended. Bass tuning machines have higher gear ratios such as 20:1 or even 28:1.

62

awkward if one breaks during a gig. A tip: You can of course pre-cut spare strings.

Locking machines

Fitting new strings is easiest with locking tuning machines. Some of these designs have a special thumbscrew to lock the string. Others have a built-in, self-actuated locking mechanism. The main advantage of locking machines is that the strings don't need to be wrapped around the tuning posts. This enhances tuning stability (see page 114).

Staggered tuning machines

To eliminate the need for string trees, which may negatively affect your instrument's sound, sustain, and tuning stability (see page 69), some guitars have *staggered* tuning machines: The tuning posts get shorter as the strings get thinner. This pulls the thin strings down, increasing their pressure on the nut, just like string trees or tilted headstocks do. (More information on string trees and tilted headstocks can be found on page 54.)

New machines

Replacing budget tuners or worn machines with good, new ones will make tuning easier and may improve tuning stability. A set of good tuning machines, made to high tolerances, typically costs

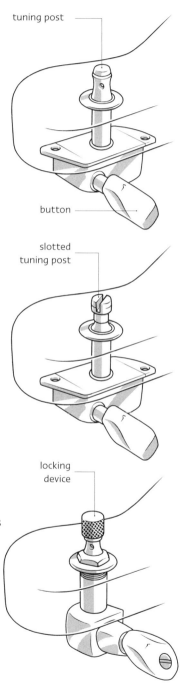

tuning post

button

slotted tuning post

locking device

A regular guitar tuning machine, a slotted ('vintage') design, and a locking machine.

63

some forty up to a hundred dollars or more for a set of gold-plated tuners with ebony knobs, for example.

Checking out machines

The strings' pitches should change at the slightest turn of the machine head buttons. If they don't, there may be play in the tuning machines — especially if it's an old or a cheap instrument. A tip: If a string binds in its slot in the nut, it won't immediately respond to the tuning machine either (see page 140).

THE BRIDGE

The bridge is the part where the strings connect to the body. The strings can be attached to the bridge itself, or to a separate tailpiece.

Tremolo or fixed

Tremolo guitars have either a *tremolo bridge* (as opposed to a *fixed bridge*) or a *tremolo tailpiece*. Both are dealt with on page 67 and onward. Non-tremolo instruments are sometimes referred to as *hard-tail guitars*.

Heavy

A bridge can be anything from a simple, bent piece of metal to a heavy, solid brass affair. The latter will help make for a fuller sound and added sustain. Some basses come with individual bridges per string.

String-through-body bridges

The term *string-through-body* (*STB*) bridge is self-explanatory. This design increases the string-to-body contact, which slightly boosts the effect that the body wood has on the sound. Also, a string-through-body bridge tends to make the sound a bit brighter, tighter (important for low B on a five- or six-string bass!), or snappier. This is a result of the slightly increased string length and the smaller string angle over the bridge saddles. Some say that STB-bridges enhance sustain as well.

64

Convertible bridges

A few instruments have a convertible bridge, which lets you either 'top-load' the strings, or attach them through the body.

Tailpieces

A tailpiece that is fixed to the top of the instrument, rather than to its tail, is commonly known as a *stop tailpiece* or *stopbar tailpiece*. Confusingly, both terms are also used to indicate bridge designs that double as tailpieces.

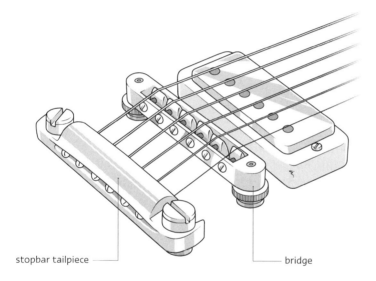

stopbar tailpiece ——————⏐   ⏐—————— bridge

Adjustments

Most guitar bridges have individual string saddles: Each string runs over a saddle, which can be adjusted in one, two, or three ways.

- The saddles can be moved lengthwise to adjust **intonation** (see page 150).

- Lowering or raising the saddles alters the **string height** (often referred to as the action; see page 146). If there are no separate saddles, the entire bridge can be raised or lowered.

- A three-dimensional adjustment allows you to adjust **string spacing** as well. This is usually seen on basses only.

65

Bass string spacing

On basses, a ⅝" (16 mm) spacing is considered narrow; wide spacings measure some ¾" (19 mm) and up. Most slapping bassists prefer a wider string spacing than finger-style players do. Basses with wider string spacing usually have wider necks too, and wider necks tend to slow down string crossings.

> ### Saddles
>
> *The saddles are often stainless steel affairs. The extra mass of big, brass saddles is said to enhance output, tone, and sustain. Some companies make synthetic saddles that increase both the instrument's sound and the strings' life expectancy.*

Floating bridge and tailpiece

Like violins, hollow-body guitars usually have a wooden, one-piece *floating bridge* that is kept in place by nothing but the strings' tension. Intonation and string height can be adjusted to a limited extent only. The *floating tailpiece*, often a prominent design in

A floating bridge, a floating wooden tailpiece, and a floating pickup (Elferink).

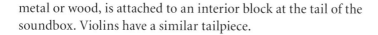

metal or wood, is attached to an interior block at the tail of the soundbox. Violins have a similar tailpiece.

Floating pickup

Some — typically up-market — hollowbodies have a *floating pickup* as well. A floating pickup is attached to the pickguard, rather than to the instrument's top. This allows the top to vibrate freely.

TREMOLO

Basically, all tremolos or *whammies* work alike. They allow you to change the tension and thus the pitch of all strings simultaneously, using an arm that is attached to a moveable bridge or tailpiece.

TIPCODE

Tipcode EGTR-003
The tremolo can be used for pitch bend and vibrato effects, as this Tipcode shows.

Pitch bend and vibrato

Technically speaking, this effect is not a tremolo. If you move the arm slowly, the resulting effect is referred to as a *pitch bend*. Smaller, faster movements generate the smaller, rapid pitch variations known as *vibrato*. Still, 'tremolo' is the most popular term for this system. *Trem*, *vibrato unit*, and *whammy* are some of the alternative names.

Synchronized tremolo

The best-known tremolo system probably is the one found on

67

the original Fender Stratocaster and many of the guitars based on that design. It's known as a *synchronized tremolo*, and it can be set up in two ways. One is with the bridge's base plate resting on the body; this allows the player to only lower string tension. More commonly, the bridge is set up so that you can also raise the strings' pitches. In this case, the bridge's base plate floats a bit above the instrument's top.

Basic, synchronized tremolo.

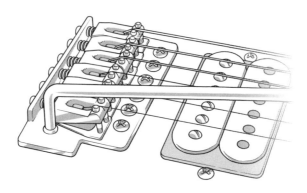

Bigsby

Another system, the Bigsby vibrato unit, features a large handle and a fixed bridge. The string tension is altered with a moving tailpiece. Guitars with this type of vibrato are used mainly in country and 1960s-style guitar bands.

Bigsby vibrato unit.

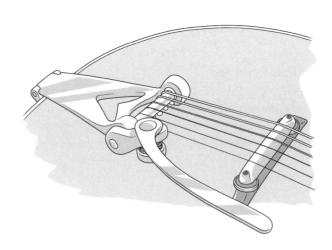

Detuning strings

Tremolos (and string bends) can cause severe tuning problems. How? When the trem arm or *whammy bar* is released, the strings may not return to their original pitch due to friction at the nut, the string trees, or the saddles. Also, using the tremolo will vary the tension on the string wraps around the tuning posts (see page 114). Another culprit? The strings' ball ends, which move back and forth in the bridge when using the tremolo, may not have returned to their original positions. A *double-locking tremolo* is the answer to these problems.

Floyd Rose

The best-known double locking tremolo bears the name of its designer, Floyd Rose. Apart from allowing for impressive pitch variations, both up and down, this type of tremolo features two locking systems. At the bridge, the strings are locked with small clamps, rather than using ball ends. At the other end, they're anchored by a *locking nut.*

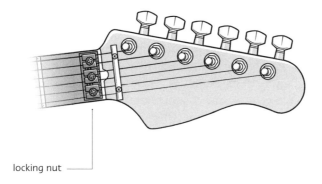

locking nut

A locking nut clamps the strings at the nut.

Clamp

A locking nut or *lock-nut* clamps the strings down at the nut, so that using the tremolo won't affect the exact position of the wraps around the tuning posts — and thus the tuning — anymore.

Fine-tuning machines

Of course, a locking nut renders the regular tuning machines useless. That's why guitars with a locking nut have *fine-tuning machines* or *fine tuners* at the bridge.

69

String changes

A locking nut makes changing strings a bit harder: You need tools for both the locking nut and the bridge clamps, and you need to cut the strings' ball ends before you can fit them. A locking nut also influences the sound, as the string sections behind the nut are cut off. With a regular nut, these sections will also vibrate.

Floyd Rose tremolo system with bridge and fine-tuning machines (Jackson).

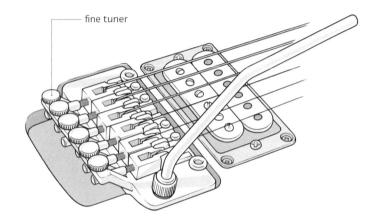

fine tuner

Dive bombing

Floyd Rose tremolos and similar designs can be found on many guitars for players who like musical dive bombing, fast and loud solos, and severe string bendings. This type of guitar usually features 24 large frets, one or more humbuckers, and a narrow, relatively flat neck with a slim (C-type) profile.

Different solutions

Rather than locking the strings at the bridge and the nut, some guitar makers prefer to make them slide more smoothly at those points, for instance by using special nuts (page 72), or string ends (bullets, rather than balls) or by getting rid of the string trees (page 54). Locking tuning machines, which were dealt with on page 63, can help prevent detuning strings by reducing or eliminating the number of wraps at the tuning posts.

Detuning

When checking out new tremolo guitars, you'll find that the strings detune quickly because they haven't stabilized yet. Also, note that when you play string bends on tremolo guitars, the pitch of the adjacent strings will change too (a result of the bent string pulling the bridge up a little). On guitars with fixed bridges, they won't.

TIP

The arm

Tremolo arms come in screw-in, pop-in, bayonet, and other versions. Some are designed to stay at your fingertips all the time. Others drop down as soon as you let go, and there are arms that can be adjusted to do either. Pop-in arms are the easiest ones to remove or attach. Check to see if the receiver is adjustable, so you won't have to deal with a trem arm that falls out spontaneously.

U-bar

If you like a trem, but don't like its arm, it's good to know that some types of tremolo can be operated — to a limited extent — with the palm of your hand. Other designs feature a U-bar instead of the traditional arm.

Less sustain?

Some experts believe that tremolo systems reduce the instrument's sustain, as the springs absorb some of the vibrations. On the other hand, there are plenty of tremolo guitars with great sustain.

Breaking strings and tremolos

If a string breaks on a tremolo guitar, the tremolo springs will make the other strings go up in pitch. In other words, you can't finish the song without retuning your instrument or replacing the broken string.

Locking your tremolo

The term *locking tremolo* is also used for tremolos that can be locked to make them behave like a fixed, hard-tail bridge. If you want to be able to lock your tremolo temporarily, some companies make little devices that simply secure the trem's arm.

71

NUTS

Most nuts are made of plastic, graphite, or metal. Hollowbody players often prefer organic materials, such as bone or fossil ivory. Bone is used on various solid-body guitars too. Metal nuts reduce the tonal difference between open and fretted strings (unless you have a zero fret), and may add a little extra brightness to the sound. Heavy metal nuts will also increase the sustain. Plastic nuts can help reduce twanginess and string buzz, but they're most likely to cause friction

Smooth
The harder and smoother a nut is, the easier tuning will be. A hard, smooth nut will also improve tuning stability: If you bend strings or use your tremolo, the strings have to be able to move through the slots without binding. High quality synthetic, carbon, or graphite nuts have been specifically designed for these purposes. Also, there are nuts with built-in rollers and ball bearings.

Slots
When switching to heavier-gauge strings, the nut's slots should be wide enough to keep them from getting stuck. The string slots shouldn't be too wide to prevent loss of energy (and thus a reduced tone) and buzzing sounds, due to strings moving sideways in the nut.

Adjustable nuts
To adjust string height, nuts can be lowered (with a file), raised (with shims), or replaced. These are basically all jobs for a professional. Only few instruments have a height-adjustable nut.

PICKUPS

The sound of a (bass) guitar depends a great deal on the pickups. After all, these are the devices that convert the notes you play to the electric signals that are eventually turned into sound. This section deals with the main characteristics of the various types of pickup, without getting too technical.

Bridge and neck pickups

Most guitars have two or three pickups: a bridge pickup or *rear pickup*, a neck pickup or *front pickup*, and often one in the middle too. Even if they're all the same, each will generate a different sound, just like hitting the strings in these various places does. Most basses have one or two pickups.

Tipcode EGTR-007

As you can hear in this Tipcode, the neck pickup makes for a smoother, cleaner sound, while the (identical!) bridge pickup promotes a twangier, edgier timbre.

TIPCODE

The difference

On a guitar with two identical pickups, the bridge pickup will produce a brighter, edgier, treblier, twangier sound, while the neck pickup generates a smoother, cleaner, warmer tone. The difference is similar to what you will hear if you play the strings of an acoustic guitar close to the bridge, and then near the neck.

Treble and Rhythm

Some pickup selectors are labeled 'treble' and 'rhythm' to indicate the bridge and neck pickups respectively, 'rhythm' referring to chord playing.

A coil and a magnet

Simply put, a pickup is a magnet with a length of thin copper wire wound around it thousands of times, known as the *coil*. When you play, the vibrating strings cause changes in the magnetic field that surrounds the magnet. The pickup converts these changes into electric signals that are sent to the amp.

73

Humbuckers

Unfortunately, pickups also pick up unwanted signals. This results in hum and noise, as you can clearly hear when you turn up the volume on some guitars. The solution, devised in 1955, was a pickup with two coils. The way these two coils are set up (for technicians: reverse polarity, reverse winding) makes them buck the hum. Their common name is taken from this pleasant feature: They're called *humbuckers*.

A humbucker with individually adjustable pole pieces (see page 87).

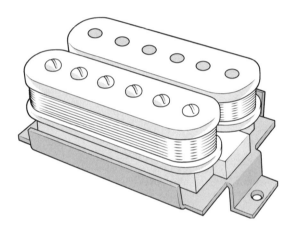

A different sound

Humbuckers sound quite different from *single-coil pickups*: fatter, beefier, meatier, warmer, broader — but also smoother and mellower. *Mini-humbuckers*, with a narrower magnetic field, produce a somewhat brighter, more open tone.

TIPCODE

Tipcode EGTR-008
The difference between single coils and humbucker is demonstrated in this Tipcode.

74

Single-coil pickups

The sound of single-coil pickups is typically described as clear, bright, tight, clean, cool, snappy, twangy, or glassy, with more bite and attack. Compared to humbuckers, single coils typically have less power and sustain.

Dummy coil

If you want the sound, but not the hum of a single-coil pickup, you can get pickups with an extra 'dummy' coil. This extra coil is meant to just buck the hum without influencing the bright sound of the main coil. Some of these noiseless *stacked pickups*, *stacks*, or *vertical humbuckers* tend to be a bit less dynamic, though.

Pickup layouts

Many guitars have humbucking or single-coil pickups only; others feature a combination of the two. Pickup layouts are often referred to by single letter combinations. For example, HSS means that the guitar has a humbucker at the bridge, followed by single-coil pickups in the middle and neck positions.

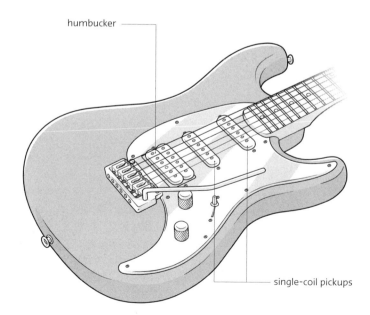

humbucker

single-coil pickups

Single-coil or humbucker?

Both single-coil and humbucking pickups are available in many different versions, and both types of pickup can be used in pretty much any style of music. The choice depends on taste, mainly, and on what you're playing. For example, with an HSS configuration you can use the humbucker for a scorching, heavily distorted solo, the middle pickup for a clean ballad, and the neck pickup for some smooth chords.

Two very well-known solid-body designs: one with two humbuckers, the other with three single-coil pickups.

Gibson Les Paul®

Fender Stratocaster®

Different types

That said, there are many different types of humbuckers, and may different types of single coil pickups. Heavy rock guitarists often use a guitar with two humbuckers, and so do most jazz players — but they don't use the same type of humbuckers.

Coil-taps and humbucking singles

On some guitars, one or both humbuckers can be used as single coils as well, so you can have the best of both worlds. A special switch (*coil-tap* or *coil-splitter*) simply disengages one of the two coils of the humbucker. Likewise, two single-coil pickups can be wired so that they behave and sound like a humbucker.

Bass pickups

Most of what has been said above goes for bass pickups too. However, single-coil pickups do not present so much of a humming problem on basses.

J or P

Many bass pickups are modeled after Fender's Jazz Bass and Precision Bass pickups. Because these are registered trademarks, the pickups of other brands are often labeled J-style and P-style, for example. The P-style pickup is a very recognizable split-coil humbucking design. It's mounted most in the middle pickup

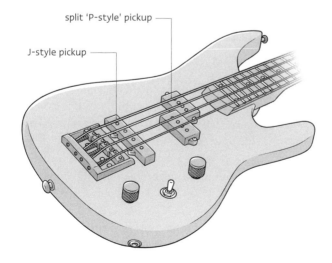

split 'P-style' pickup

J-style pickup

Two popular types of bass pickups.

position (basses don't have pickups close to the neck) and provides a low, fat, rock type of sound. On basses, bridge pickups produce more of a midrange, growling type of sound.

TONE AND VOLUME

Most guitars and basses have very plain, basic tone and volume controls. They must be well-placed, feel smooth and solid, and work evenly throughout their entire rotation.

How many
Some players prefer an instrument with just one shared volume control and one shared tone control for all pickups; others like more options. If you have a volume control for each pickup, you can blend their sounds rather than just choose one or the other. Likewise, having a tone control for each pickup allows you to create different sounds, and to change from one to the other by using the pickup selector only.

Tone control
Tone controls on guitars and basses are usually *treble cut* models. When they're fully open, the sound is at its brightest. Turning them counterclockwise will cut the higher (treble) frequencies, gradually making the sound darker or thicker.

Volume control
On many instruments, the volume control affects the tone as well: If you reduce the volume, the treble is cut too, to some extent. This is one reason why many (bass)guitarists audition their instruments with all controls wide open: It allows them to hear everything there is. The treble-cut effect of a volume control can sometimes be eliminated by having your guitar technician install a capacitor.

More controls
There are many more types of tone controls available, ranging from five-step frequency range switches to active midrange boosters, or

78

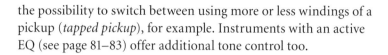

the possibility to switch between using more or less windings of a pickup (*tapped pickup*), for example. Instruments with an active EQ (see page 81–83) offer additional tone control too.

Balance control
Rather than a pickup selector, most basses have a balance control that allows you to choose one pickup or the other, or a blend of both. Alternatively, they have a volume control for each pickup. Balance controls often have a center detent, so you can 'feel' its middle position.

Potentiometer
The technical term for the devices that are controlled with the volume and tone knobs is potentiometer or pot.

TIP

Output jack
The signal from the pickup(s) leaves your instrument at the output jack. As this is where you plug *in* your cable, it is often — mistakenly — referred to as an *input*. A tip: Worn output jacks can be a source of noise. They can be easily replaced.

PICKUP SELECTORS

The pickup selector or toggle switch allows you to choose which pickup(s) you use — but there's more.

Three-way
Most guitars with two pickups have a three-way toggle switch, allowing you to choose either the bridge pickup (position 1), both pickups (2), or the neck pickup (3).

Five-way
If your guitar has three pickups, it'll usually have a five-way

79

Guitar with
a three-way
toggle
switch.

toggle switch

selector: bridge pickup (position 1), bridge and middle pickups (position 2), middle (3), middle and neck (4), neck pickup (5).

Humbucking single-coils
On some guitars, the selector has a position that makes two single-coil pickups behave like a humbucker. (For technicians: This requires the middle pickup to have reverse winding and reverse polarity.)

In series or in parallel
Usually, the two coils of a humbucker are connected *in series*. On some guitars you can use humbuckers *in parallel* too, with a flick of the pickup selector. Without getting too technical, this means that they start behaving like single coils, with a glassier, brighter, clearer sound, and a reduced output.

80

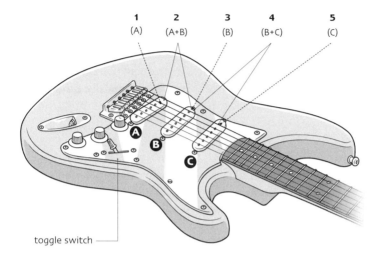

This is how a regular five-way pickup selecto works.

A = bridge pickup
B = middle pickup
C = neck pickup

toggle switch

Out of phase

The two coils of a humbucker are traditionally wired in phase. On some guitars, the pickup selector offers an out of phase setting too. This makes for a thin, frail sound with little output that's often severely boosted, or used for specific effects.

TIP

Solo? Direct out!

For solos, most players use the bridge pickup, and tone and volume controls are wide open. A *direct-out switch* gets you there immediately. It sends the bridge pickup's signal directly to the amp, and bypasses tone and volume controls (so they behave as if they're open).

ACTIVE BASSES

Active basses are instruments with active electronics, powered by a built-in battery. They produce a hotter signal (that's why bass amps usually have a separate — lower sensitivity — input for active instruments). An essential difference with *passive* instruments is that the active circuitry allows you additional control over your tone. On a passive instrument you can only cut certain frequencies, while active instruments typically allow you to cut and *boost* three separate frequency ranges (bass, mid, and treble)

Parametric

Apart from this *three-band tone control*, you can usually choose the exact midrange frequency you want to cut or boost. This is known as a *swept EQ* or *parametric mid EQ* (equalizer).

An active EQ provides additional tonal variation. Stacked knobs save space.

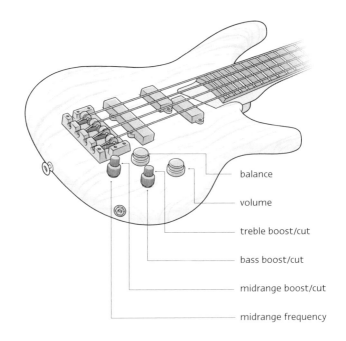

balance

volume

treble boost/cut

bass boost/cut

midrange boost/cut

midrange frequency

Less noise, more output

Basses with active electronics can be used with long cables without any loss in sound or dynamics (see page 118). To cope with the enhanced output of the active preamp, most bass amplifiers have a separate 'active' input.

82

Battery

The built-in preamplifier is usually powered by one or two 9-volt batteries. These can last up to two or three thousand playing hours, provided you don't forget to unplug your instrument cable when you're done playing. (Unplugging it turns the preamp off.)

Active or passive?

Active basses are often said to sound tighter, cleaner, and more focused, but less organic, warm, or lively than passive basses. That said, many active basses have a switch to bypass the active electronics, turning the instrument into a passive bass. Do note that active basses without that option can't do without a battery!

TIP

Little variation

Some of the most popular passive basses offer very little tonal variation — especially older models — but they happen to produce a sound that works well for many bassists, and for many styles of music. Active basses, with their extended tone controls, are often unable to reproduce that characteristic passive sound.

Optional

On some basses, the active circuitry is an option, usually costing some hundred to two hundred dollars extra.

MORE TYPES OF PICKUPS

There are many more types of pickups than the ones described above. Here are some examples.

Active pickups

Both guitars and basses can be provided with active pickups, which have a weaker type of magnet and less windings than

83

passive pickups. The resulting lower output is boosted by a built-in preamp.

The difference

Active pickups provide a clean, noise-free, high-output signal, which works great with multi-effect devices, or for players who want a heavily distorted sound without losing definition or clarity, and without feedback. Also, string pull (page 86) is never a problem. Advocates of passive pickups, however, often claim that active pickups tend to sound a bit too clean, and lack dynamics.

 TIP

Expensive

Passive pickups are still the industry standard. In part, this is due to the price of active pickups. A note: Most active bass guitars have passive pickups. These basses are called 'active' because of their active preamp and EQ.

Piezo pickups

Some basses and a few guitars have additional non-magnetic *piezo pickups* (see page 168). These pickups are similar to the ones used on electric-acoustic guitars. On electric guitars, they generate a bright, clear, 'acoustic' type of sound. On basses, they're said to help produce a big, deep sound with lots of bright definition, which is generally more useful for solos and playing chords than for regular bass parts.

Invisible

Piezo pickups are usually built invisibly into the bridge. To get a balanced sound, the gain can be adjusted per string, using one pickup for each string and individual *trim pots* in one of the body cavities. On some instruments, the balance between the piezo and the magnetic pickups can be set too. Others have dual outputs: one for the each type of pickup, so you can choose to use different types of amps too.

And furthermore...

84

... there are special pickups that allow for infinite sustain; pickups

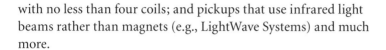

with no less than four coils; and pickups that use infrared light beams rather than magnets (e.g., LightWave Systems) and much more.

WINDINGS, MAGNETS, AND MORE

Knowing a little more about pickups can make it easier to find the guitar or bass of your choice, or to select replacement pickups for your instrument.

Wrap wire

Pickups vary in tone and output as a result of numerous variables. One of the most obvious parameters is the number of windings. More wrap wire make for a 'hotter pickup' with a higher output; more mids, but less high end; and a warmer, darker (but less clear or transparent) tone.

By hand or by machine

There's even a difference between hand-wound and machine-wound pickups. Hand-wound models typically promote a genuine vintage tone, with more of a complex, live sound — just like hand-hammered cymbals sound different from machine-hammered cymbals; ask your drummer. Another difference between the two may very well be that pickup makers who go for hand winding simply use higher quality parts. Machine-wound pickups are more consistent — and some players like that, while others don't.

Lead or rhythm

The hotter a pickup, the easier it will be to create overdriven sounds and infinite sustain. Solo guitarists typically prefer hot pickups, while chords often sound better using lower output pickups.

Type of magnet

Pickups use different types of magnets. The most common types are Alnico 2 (II), Alnico 5 (V), and ceramic magnets. Alnico 2 is often said to promote a warm, dark tone. Alnico 5 is frequently used for pickups that are designed for a brighter sound and a higher output. Ceramic magnets help contribute to a very transparent, snappier, brighter (if you like it) or edgier, harsher (if you don't) sound with a strong attack.

Immaterial

However, there are experts who claim that magnet material isn't that crucial at all. After all, there are very warm sounding ceramic pickups.

Pickups and prices

Budget instruments often lack expressiveness and tonal richness, which can be due to the use of cheaper (ceramic, ferrite, or other non-Alnico) pickups. Some guitars in the two-hundred-dollar price range do come with Alnico pickups, though. Likewise, some professional instruments have ceramic pickups for an aggressive, in-your-face tone.

String pull

If a pickup with a strong magnet is too close to the strings, it may actually pull on them. This phenomenon, *string pull*, can cause anything from undesirable overtones to buzzing strings, loss of sustain, and out-of-tune notes.

The common solution is to adjust the pickup a bit farther away from the strings (see page 154). Guitars with *high-impedance pickups* are more sensitive to string pull than instruments with (usually active) *low-impedance pickups.*

Single bar or individual pole pieces

Most pickups have as many *pole pieces* as they have strings. When you bend your strings, the signal may decrease as the strings are pushed toward the 'dead spots' between the pole pieces. Using pickups with a single magnetic *bar* or *blade* solves this problem. Bar pickups typically produce a less percussive attack and a stronger sustain.

86

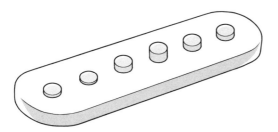

Adjustable, staggered, or flat

There are pickup designs that allow you to adjust the height of each pole piece for a balanced output per string. Also, there are pickups available with either *level* or *staggered pole pieces* — and there are guitars that offer a choice between the two.

The difference

If you replace a flat-pole pickup by a staggered design, the result will be a slightly different tonal balance from string to string. Generally speaking, though, staggered-magnet pickups work better with guitars with arched (low radius) fingerboards, while flat-pole designs tend to yield better results when used on instruments with modern, flatter, high-radius fingerboards.

Soaked in wax

At high volume levels, pickups can act like microphones and produce feedback. To prevent this, good pickups are soaked in a potting solution (e.g., wax).

Pickup covers

Pickups often have nicknames based on the looks of their protective covers. Lipstick pickups have a (fake) lipstick tube cover, and a soapbar pickup has a broad rectangular cover.

TIP

Metal, plastic, nothing

Metal covers influence the magnetic field, of course, unlike plastic pickup covers. If you'd have two identical pickups, one with a metal cover, the other with a plastic (or no) cover, the first would sound a bit less bright, and have a somewhat smaller dynamic range. A tip: Leave removing or replacing pickup covers to a technician.

Right angle or offset

Many instruments have the bridge pickup not at a right angle to the strings, but slightly offset. This makes the treble strings sound a bit brighter, with a little extra bite: Having their pole pieces closer to the bridge makes them sound as if you were playing them closer to the bridge.

Guitars and synthesizers

Electric guitars and basses can be linked to synthesizers, sequencers, and other electronic equipment. This requires a special type of pickup, often referred to as a *divider pickup*, *MIDI pickup*, or *hex pickup*. The pickup sends its signals either directly to a dedicated guitar synthesizer, or to a converter that can be hooked up to the huge variety of electronic instruments and equipment that features MIDI (Musical Instrument Digital Interface).

REPLACING PICKUPS

Most guitarists and bassists would rather buy another instrument than replace their pickups, but it can't hurt to consider the second option as a cost-effective way to improve your sound. Prices of good aftermarket pickups typically range from some thirty to a hundred dollars and more.

On CD

The problem in choosing pickups is that you can't just try them out on your own instrument. Instead, you have to rely on your salesperson's advice and on the description pickup makers supply you with in their catalogs. A few companies present all their pickups on CD — but then you still don't know how they sound in *your* instrument and with *your* amp. That said, there are — very few — guitars that feature an interchangeable pickup system, allowing you to use different combinations of various types of pickups.

Technical data

Some catalogs and websites provide you with tons of technical data that may help you choose a pickup. For example, a higher *DC resistance* can indicate a higher output and a fatter sound; the height of a pickup's *resonant peak* may tell you about its clarity of sound (higher is brighter). Do note that it takes quite a bit of additional knowledge and experience to translate this information into sound, and that you ears typically tell you more than such data.

Enhance or compensate

New pickups can enhance certain characteristics of your instrument, or compensate for them. For example, you can buy pickups that make your guitar sound a bit brighter or twangier. Likewise, guitar and bass makers may combine brighter sounding woods with warmer sounding pickups, for instance. Want a vintage sound? Some companies produce special pickups that help you recreate that warm, smooth timbre.

Radius and string spacing, neck or bridge

New pickups should match your instrument's design. For example, there are pickups for wider and narrower string spacings, and pickups that have been designed to match either flatter or more curved fingerboards. Some pickup designs require separate left- and right-hand versions (the pickups being dissimilar for the low- and the high-pitched strings). Others are designed for use either in neck or bridge positions only (the latter usually being stronger to make up for the smaller string movement near the bridge), or in both positions.

Rewiring

You can customize your instrument by having it rewired (to add to or change the options your pickup selector offers you, for example), or by having a volume potentiometer with a different value installed (the lower the value, the darker the sound), or by

89

many other operations that require the use of a soldering gun and more knowledge of electronics than you'll get from this book. Some companies offer their guitars with a choice of wiring options.

AUDITIONING INSTRUMENTS

In the end, choosing an instrument is all about playing it. Here are some pointers.

Avoid damage
First of all, avoid damaging the instruments you play-test with belt buckles, zippers, and other metal parts of your clothing.

Well-adjusted
You can judge instruments only if they're well-adjusted: action, neck, pickup height, intonation. Please refer to Chapter 10 for more information.

Pro instruments
Even if your budget is limited, it can't hurt to include some professional instruments in your quest: Knowing what great instruments sound, feel, and play like will also help you to find the best instrument that your budget allows for.

Too many guitars
Selecting instruments gets less confusing if you don't compare too many of them at a time. So pick out three guitars or basses, based on the salesperson's advice or your own ears or eyes, and play them for a while. Then swap the one you like least for another instrument. Listen again. And so on, until you've found the one you're looking for.

Too many things
Also, don't compare too many things at a time. If, for example, you use the neck pickup most of the time, compare various instruments using the neck pickup only. Try out other options

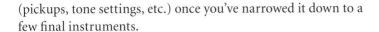

(pickups, tone settings, etc.) once you've narrowed it down to a few final instruments.

One amp
Use one amp only. If not, you're comparing amps as much as you're comparing instruments: Every amplifier has its own sound. Also bring your own instrument, if you have one, so you can use it as a reference. You may even want to bring your own amp, as it is such a crucial element of your sound.

Which amp
If bringing your own amp is not an option, use a similar one. Keep from experimenting with other amps — and effects — until you've limited your choice to a few instruments. If you're buying both a guitar and an amp, it's usually wisest to start with the guitar, and then look for an amp that stresses, completes, perfects, or enhances the instrument's sound.

Clean
Consider playing all instruments 'clean' first. This tells you a lot more about their true character than using overdrive channels and effects. Likewise, it's a good idea to have all volume and tone controls fully open. If you're comparing active bass guitars, set their tone controls to their 'neutral' center detents.

TIP

Acoustically
Even if they're solidbodies, it's good to judge instruments acoustically as well. What a bass or guitar sounds like unamplified will tell you a lot about its character and sonic properties. Listen to the instrument's timbre, play all positions at the fingerboard and listen for sustain (and dead spots...), and listen to everything else mentioned in this chapter. If you press your ear against the body, you'll be able to hear every nuance. When you're choosing a hollow-body guitar, it's even more important to also judge it acoustically.

91

More and more

Once you're left with a few instruments to choose from, play them longer and try out all pickup selector settings, tone and volume controls, and anything else you need to assess their quality and sound potential.

Balance

Playing along the fingerboard and across the strings can bring out the instrument's balance in volume, timbre, and sustain. For example, the thinner strings will always sound shorter and brighter than the thicker strings, but they shouldn't sound as if they were mounted on different instruments.

Dynamics and response

Play the strings as soft as you will in performance, and see if the instrument responds immediately. Play as loud as you ever will (or as loud as the store owner allows you to), and check if the instrument holds up.

Good guitars and basses have a large dynamic range, i.e., they respond well to playing softly and can handle loud playing just as well. Of course, this is not relevant for instruments that are specifically designed for loud music.

Timbre

Guitarists and bassists use thousands of words and expressions to indicate an instrument's timbre or character, and there are thousands of things you can listen for. What's important to you mainly depends on the music you want to use the instrument for, and on your personal taste, of course: a bright or a dark sound, major transparency or massive power, screaming or smooth highs, thick or crunchy mids, punchy or warm lows, a smooth or a percussive midrange.

Versatility

While many guitars and basses have been designed with a specific sound or style of music in mind, others were built to offer lots of versatility. Still, you can't always expect to find everything you want in one single bass or guitar. This is just one of the reasons why many artists use more than one instrument onstage.

Everything

Set-in necks are said to promote sustain. And yes, many guitars with set-in necks do have an impressive sustain. But these guitar designs often have thicker bodies too, and thicker necks, and they don't have a tremolo… The message: How an instrument sounds is always the combined result of all its components — so listen to the entire instrument, and not to its parts.

The same?

Finally: No two guitars or basses sound and play exactly the same, not even if they're the same make and series. So always play an instrument before you buy it, and don't accept an 'identical' one from the stockroom.

SECONDHAND

If you buy a secondhand instrument, there are quite a few things that need special attention.

*   Examine the body, neck, and fingerboard for **cracks** and other damage.

*   Small cracks in **the finish** (*finish checking*) can be caused by age, but also by sudden changes in air humidity. Have an expert look at the instrument.

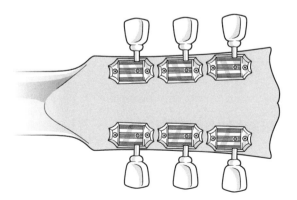

Check the tuning machines…

- Check the **tuning machines** for play. They should only rotate, and not be able to move up and down or sideways. Also, even the slightest turn should alter a string's pitch (provided the string doesn't bind in its slot in the nut).

- If the tuning machines **squeak**, a tiny drop of oil may help. New machines can be fitted if necessary. A set of high quality tuners will usually set you back some forty dollars or more. This doesn't include having them installed.

- **Rattles and buzzes** can be the result of bad adjustment, loose string windings, loose pickguard or adjustment screws, a worn nut, worn frets...

- Check **the frets** for dents and flat spots: Worn frets can result in buzzes and out-of-tune notes. Dented frets hamper string-bending. The solution is to have the frets leveled or to have the instrument refretted — which is expensive.

- Check the **pickups and the pickup selector**. Hook up the instrument and press the strings down so that they touch the pickups, one by one, or use a small metal object (such as a paperclip). You should hear a click every time you hit a pickup. Check all the pickups in all selector settings.

- If tone and volume controls are **scratchy**, the *potentiometers* or *pots* may need to be cleaned (see page 146) or replaced. If they're just dirty, the noise should fade a little when you rotate them a few times.

- Especially when buying privately, it may pay off to have the instrument **appraised**. Vintage instruments should be checked to see if they're truly vintage all over.

DEVELOPMENTS

Though most popular guitar and bass designs have been around for decades, there will always be room for innovation. Not a year goes by without the introduction of new features and ideas.

Modeling guitars

In 2002, Line 6 introduced the modeling guitar, the Variax. The instruments uses advanced modeling technology to emulate the sounds of twenty-five classic electric and acoustic guitars, available at the turn of a knob.

More

A growing number of companies have introduced guitars with a variety of digital features ever since, allowing you to:

- **Switch guitar sounds** without switching instruments.

- Use **different tunings** without even looking at your tuning machines; simply select the one you want, and play.

- Make your six-string guitar sound like a **twelve-string**.

- Connect your guitar to **your computer** using a simple USB cable, for jamming, recording, or pod-casting (but note that you can connect any electric guitar to a computer's USB port with a special plug/preamp combination, e.g., the Stealth Plug).

- Use an **acoustic guitar** to play electric sounds, with onboard reverb and distortion (e.g., the Ibanez Montage).

- And there's **more to come**.

Separate outputs

If you want to use an acoustic amp for the acoustic sounds of your digital guitar, it's handy if the instrument has separate outputs for an acoustic and an electric amp.

95

6

Good Strings

Strings should be easy to play, sound good, and last long, preferably without being too expensive.

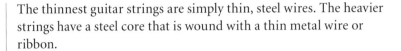

The thinnest guitar strings are simply thin, steel wires. The heavier strings have a steel core that is wound with a thin metal wire or ribbon.

Differences
There's generally not too much difference in the sound of plain strings, from brand to brand. The wound strings show much bigger differences, and the material of the wrap wire is one of the reasons why. The three most common windings are nickel-plated steel, pure nickel, and pure (stainless) steel.

Nickel-plated steel
Most guitarists use strings with a nickel-plated steel wrap. Confusingly, these are usually referred to as nickel-wound.

Pure nickel
Strings with a solid nickel wrap are commonly known as pure nickel-wound. This type of string, which was especially popular in the 1950s and 1960s, produces a warmer, richer, vintage type of sound. Chrome contributes to a mellow tone.

Steel
Steel-wound strings sound the brightest, with a lot of cutting power. Also, steel wrap wire can be a good choice if you have very acidic perspiration (see page 108).

TIP

The core
Some string manufacturers use a hexagonal core for their wound strings to provide better grip for the winding. Others prefer the traditional round core, stating that this produces a more even, truer tone.

Heavy and light
When you buy a set of strings, you can choose between various gauges. Here are the main characteristics of light-gauge and heavy-gauge string sets.

Light-gauge strings	Heavy-gauge strings
'lighter,' edgier, and twangier tone	'heavier,' fatter, more solid tone
don't sustain as long	longer sustain
have less volume	have a higher output
are easier to play and to bend	make playing a bit heavier
break more easily	last longer

The main differences.

010

A set of guitar strings is always referred to by the gauge of the thinnest string. These gauges are given in fractions of an inch. An 010 string measures 0.010" (0.25 mm).

Which gauge?

On solid-body guitars, 009s and 010s are the most popular choice, and you can get 0095s too (known as Light Plus, for example). As heavier-gauge strings produce more tone, many players prefer to use the heaviest strings they still feel comfortable with, which is also a matter of getting used to them, of course.
On the other hand, some guitars really do sound better with a lighter set.

	1st string	6th string
Extra Light, Ultra Light	008 (0.20 mm)	038 (0.95 mm)
Light	009	042
Regular	010	046
Medium	011	052
Heavy/Jazz	012 (0.30 mm)	054 (1.4 mm)

Examples of bass string gauges.

Names and numbers

Most manufacturers use names as well as numbers to indicate the gauges of their string sets. Above are some of the commonly used names and gauges. The gauges of the sixth strings are examples: They may vary per brand or type of string, as may the gauges of the other four strings.

99

W = Wound

The thinner sets usually have a plain third string (G), whereas most thicker sets have a wound G. Wound third strings are usually indicated with a W (i.e., 020W). Some players prefer a wound G in light-gauge sets too, as they tend to have better tone and intonation. Various brands offer light-gauge wound Gs as single strings.

Light top/heavy bottom

Some players like to combine light-gauge treble strings (making string bends easier) with heavier wound strings (for a fat, strong bass sound). Such light top/heavy bottom sets are readily available.

Different strings?

If you've switched from one type of string or string gauge to another, be sure to check if your instrument needs adjustment. For example, heavier-gauge strings pull harder on the neck (raising the action) and the tremolo springs. Switching string brands may require adjustments as well, even if you're still using the same gauge: The strings of some brands have a higher tension than equally heavy strings from another make.

Heavier gauge

Changing to heavier-gauge strings may also cause tuning problems: The thicker strings can get caught in the nut's slots. The solution is to have the slots widened or to have the nut replaced.

Thicker core

Wound strings of a certain gauge may vary in how stiff they feel from brand to brand. You can even feel this difference without putting them on your instrument. A stiffer string will probably have a thicker core, making for a higher output, a heavier feel, and a better sustain than a string with a thinner core. More flexible, thin core strings are often easier to play, sound sweeter, keep their tone longer, and have better intonation. Core thickness can vary per brand and per series.

Flat or round

Most wound strings are wrapped with a round wire. Others have a flat ribbon winding. These *flat-wound* strings are mostly used by jazz players (usually 012s or even 013s), but also by surf guitarists, for example. They promote a warm, mellow, rounded, subdued tone, and produce less finger noise than the brighter-sounding *roundwounds*. Their sustain is shorter, and so is their life-expectancy: The metal 'tape' wears down faster than round wrap wire does. Conversely, flat-wound strings help extend fret life.

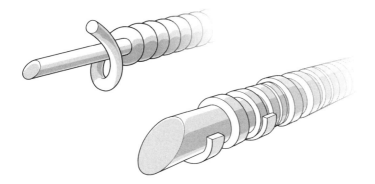

Round-wound and flat-wound strings.

Half-rounds
If you can't decide between flat-wound and round-wound strings, you may try *halfrounds* or *groundwounds*, which offer a bit of both worlds: some or most of the brighter sound of roundwounds, and the smooth feel of flat-wound strings, as well as their reduced finger noise and fret wear. *Compound-wound strings* have multiple layers of winding.

BASS STRINGS

Bass strings are always wound. The extra mass of the winding allows them to sound as low as they do.

Flat or round
Bass strings come with the same wrap wire variations as guitar strings (see above):

101

- **Roundwounds** are by far the most popular choice.

- **Flatwounds** are mainly used by jazz, reggae, and country bass players, and sometimes in other styles as well, including metal. They produce a strong fundamental tone with reduced sustain.

- If round-wound strings sound too bright, and flatwounds have not enough sustain, you may try a set of **half-round strings.**

- For fretless basses, there are strings with a **synthetic winding** (e.g., nylon) that reduces fingerboard wear. The tape winding also makes for a smooth feel and a deep, full sound.

Gauges

Most bassists use $^{040}/_{100}$ or $^{045}/_{105}$ string sets. (The numbers refer to the gauges of the first and the fourth strings).

- The **lighter gauge strings** are generally preferred for slapping techniques, a brighter tone, and a faster attack

- The **heavier strings** provide more depth, low end, and punch.

The low B of a five- or six-string bass set usually ranges from .120 to .135.

Examples of bass string gauges.

	1st string (G)	4th string (E)
Extra Light	030 (0.75 mm)	085 (2.1 mm)
Light	035	090
Medium	040	095, 100 or 105
Medium Heavy	045	105
Heavy	050 (1.25 mm)	110 (2.8 mm)

Different scales, different strings

Bass strings come in short, medium, long, and extra-long scale versions. If you put 'standard' long-scale strings on a shorter-scale instrument, their tension will be too low, resulting in a weak tone. Besides, fitting them in the tuning posts can be a problem.

CHOOSING YOUR STRINGS

Choosing strings, no matter how much you know about them, is mainly a matter of trying out lots of different types. In this process, it can help to jot down your comments on every new set of strings you try out. There's room to do so on page 241.

The sound
A certain type of string may sound great on one guitar, and less so on another. It may also sound great when you play it, and not if someone else does. The right choice depends on the instrument, your style of playing, your personal preferences, and so on.

Listen
How do you judge strings? By listening to their tone, but also by paying attention to their output and dynamic range, to how fast they respond, and to how responsive they are to the nuances of your playing. Also, listen if the set is balanced from string to string, in terms of volume and tone.

From set to set
One of the reasons players tend to spend a little more on strings is that good strings are consistent from set to set: Each set of strings provides the same results.

Low B

TIP

For five- and six-string bassists, low B usually is the most critical string. Even at this low pitch — when played open — this string should produce a tight, focused, well-defined sound.

String life
When strings get older, their sound gets duller and their intonation will suffer: They don't sound in tune over their entire

range anymore. Also, they become harder to tune, and more likely to break. For an optimal performance, there are players who put on a new set of strings before each gig. Others, with less critical ears, less critical equipment, or less money, play the same strings for half a year or longer. And every time they do replace them, they're surprised by how bright their instrument can sound.

A month

If you play some eight to ten hours a week, try replacing your strings after two to four weeks. Do the new ones sound noticeably brighter? Then you may try replacing them sooner next time. If you don't hear a difference, keep the next set on for four to six weeks, and see what happens. Another guideline: When they discolor, wound strings are usually past their best. They may not break for years, but a new set will improve your sound.

Bassists

Bass players use their strings longer than most guitarists. If you slap a lot and if you want a bright, funky, percussive sound for that purpose, you may want to replace yours much more often.

String care

The more you play, the more acidic your sweat, and the thinner your strings, the shorter they will last. You can make strings last longer by taking good care of them, as you will read in the next chapter.

Coated strings

Various companies make strings with a special type of coating that protects them from the influence of sweat, dust, and moisture. Their higher price pays for a longer life span, depending on, among other things, your chemical makeup. Coated strings are sometimes said to sound and feel different — but opinions differ, and much has changed since these strings first hit the market. Trying them out is the only way to see how they sound and feel to you.

Spare sets

The more often you change your strings, the less likely they are to give up on you unexpectedly. On the other hand, even a brand new string can break at the first chord. So always take one or two spare sets with you. High E-strings break most often, and some strings sets come with two of them.

Broken strings

If a plain string breaks, you can often replace just that one string. Replacing a single wound string will disturb the tonal balance of the strings: The new one sounds much brighter than the ones you've been playing for a while.

How much?

Most guitar strings cost between five to eight dollars a set, but there are sets that cost twenty dollars or more. Bass string prices typically range from about twenty to forty or fifty dollars. Some companies provide much cheaper strings. Will the cheap ones work for you, or are the expensive ones more cost-effective, or do they simply sound so much better that you happily spend the extra money?

Packaging

Some companies use corrosion-inhibiting envelopes to package each string individually; others save the environment (and money) by using a single box or envelope for a set.

Brands

Examples of well-known string brands are Black Diamond, D'Addario, D'Aquisto, Darco, Dean Markley, DR, Elixir, Ernie Ball, GHS, LaBella, Rotosound, SIT, and Thomastik-Infeld. A few makes concentrate on bass or jazz strings, for example, but most of them make all kinds of strings. Quite a few makers also produce strings for other companies and brands. For example, many guitar and bass companies have their own strings, but they usually buy these strings elsewhere.

7

Cleaning and Changing Strings

To get the best out of your instrument, you'll need to pay some extra attention to your strings — and that doesn't take much time or effort. Keeping them clean and fitting them properly is basically all there is to it.

The cleaner you keep your strings, the longer they will sound good. Clean strings also will help keep your fingerboard clean.

Perspiration

First of all, it really helps if you play with clean, dry hands only. Using a pH-neutral soap may reduce perspiration. If you sweat heavily, try rubbing your hands with talcum powder before you play. Don't use too much to prevent the powder from gumming up the wound strings and killing their tone.

Afterwards

No matter how clean your hands are, your fingers will leave natural oils and perspiration on your strings, so wipe them with a clean, dry, lint-free cloth (an old T-shirt, for example) when you're done playing. If you have more acidic perspiration, lightly moisten the cloth with isopropyl alcohol (70% or up; the higher the percentage, the quicker it will evaporate).

Fingerboard

Don't forget to clean the underside of the strings too. Pull the cloth between the strings and the fingerboard, and run it up and down a couple of times. This also keeps the fingerboard and the frets from getting dirty, which saves time in maintenance.

String cleaners

You can make your strings last longer by using one of the many string cleaners available. These cleaners often leave a thin dirt-, oil-, and sweat-repellent film on the strings. Silicone-based cleaners also make your strings feel smoother. Other string products are specifically designed for that purpose. Before using

TIP

A different brand or winding

If string cleaners and special coatings (see page 104) don't help to reduce the effect your perspiration has on your strings, try using strings with another type of winding (see page 98), or experiment with different brands or series.

any of these products, always read the instructions carefully. Most string cleaners shouldn't get on your instrument, so slide a piece of cardboard under your strings when applying them.

Wound strings

Some players clean their wound strings by carefully pulling them up a little and then letting them snap back against the fingerboard a couple of times. This can help to get rid of gunk in the grooves of the windings.

Boiling strings

Many bass players clean their (expensive!) strings by boiling them for a few minutes, with or without a bit of vinegar, soda, detergent, or dishwashing liquid added to the water. Always rinse the strings well with plenty of cold water before getting them out of the pan: They do get extremely hot. Then dry them carefully in order to prevent oxidation.

Boiled strings may break easier, not because they have been boiled, but because there may be kinks at the ends where they were attached to the tuning posts.

Your instrument

To get your strings to last as long as possible, you need to take care of your instrument too. Rough spots on frets, or sharp edges at the nut or saddles, can cause excessive string wear. Some micro-fine sandpaper (2000 grit) may be all you need to smooth things out.

Steel wool

Don't use steel wool, as bits of the 'wool' can migrate to the instrument's pickups where they can cause a variety of problems. Another tip: Leave precision jobs to your technician.

Check your strings

Oxidized and dirty strings can easily go out of tune, as do strings that have flat spots where they cross the frets — so they should be replaced. Check your strings from time to time, and run a finger underneath them too. If you want to release the string tension for that purpose, you may need to stabilize them again afterwards (see page 114–115).

109

REPLACING STRINGS

There are lots of ways to fit new strings. Whichever one you choose, as long as you do it right, tuning stability will improve.

One by one
When putting on a new set of strings, it's usually best to change the strings one by one. This allows you to tune each new string to the one next to it, assuming that the instrument was — at least roughly — in tune to start with.

Floating bridge
On guitars with a floating bridge, replacing the strings one by one also keeps the bridge in its proper position. If the bridge position changes, even ever so slightly, your intonation will be off (see page 150–153).

All at once, or two by two
If the fingerboard needs a thorough cleaning, it may be easier to take all the strings off. Alternatively, you can replace the strings two by two. This creates sufficient room for basic cleaning purposes.

On the table
Replacing strings is easiest when your guitar is on a table or a workbench. A piece of foam plastic or a towel underneath the instrument prevents scratches and keeps it from sliding away. Washing your hands before you start helps extend string life.

Removing strings
Here's how you remove strings:

- **Unwind the first string** you want to replace (usually high E or low E), and take it off the tuning post. A string winder speeds up the process.

- To prevent the string from causing any damage when removing it at the other end, you can cut it close to the bridge. Strings should be **completely slack** before you cut them!

- If you have to remove the strings through slots in a plate on the back of the instrument, it's usually easiest to **remove the plate**. Leave it off to install the new strings, and then put it back on.

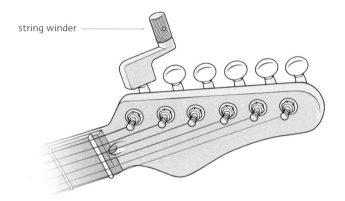

string winder

At the bridge

Feed each new string through the bridge or the stopbar tailpiece, and make sure its ball-end is in its proper position. Some types of bridges require that the ball-ends are cut off: The strings are locked with clamps.

At the tuning machines

On most electric guitars, there's a hole in the side of each tuning post (top row, next page).

1. Turn the post so that the hole faces the string, and feed the string into the hole.

2. Move the string over and around the post once.

3. Start winding the string. Make sure there are no overlapping windings (Overlapping windings reduce tuning stability!). On regular posts, make sure the string now runs underneath the hole.

4. When winding, keep the string under a little tension so it won't move at the bridge. Use your index finger to guide it through the slot in the nut, as clearly shown in the illustration on page 113.

111

This is how you attach strings to regular and slotted tuning posts.

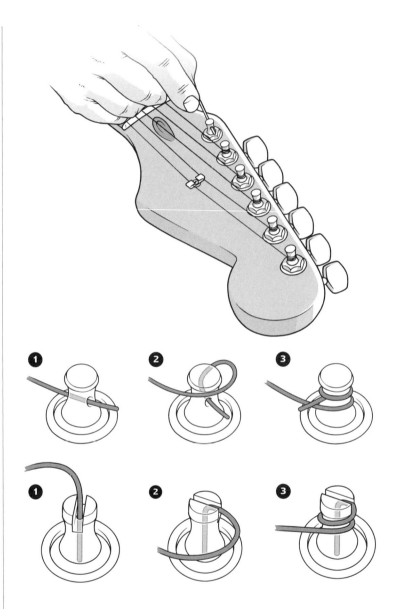

Slotted machines

Most bass guitars and some guitars have slotted tuning machines, shown above on the bottom row. They usually require you to cut the string to length before fitting it. (Only a few models allow feeding the string all the way through the posts.) For guitars, cut

Tipcode EGTR-009
This Tipcodes shows you how to put on a new string.

each string an inch and a half beyond its post. Bass strings need a little more slack. Stick the end in the hole, move it around the post once, and start winding the string. Some players feed the string through the slot once more after the first winding.

The tuning posts should turn in the direction of the arrow.

Less wraps, more stability

Contrary to what many players believe, the number of wraps around the tuning post should be kept to a minimum: More wraps will reduce tuning stability. How come? When you bend your strings or ride the trem bar, the tension on the wraps changes. When you let go of the string or the trem bar, the wraps may not get back to their original position. The more wraps, the larger chances are that they don't. As a result, the string(s) will detune. As a rule of thumb, try to stick to a maximum of two wraps.

Locking machines

If you have locking tuning machines, the strings don't need to be wrapped around the posts at all, thus improving tuning stability. Bringing the strings to pitch usually requires less than one full turn of the tuning post.

TIP

Too long

Most strings are way too long when you buy them. You can cut them once they're in place, or before installing them, at about two inches past the tuning post. On traditional slotted tuning machines, you have to cut the strings to length beforehand. In other words: You will need a wire-cutter to replace strings, so always bring one in your instrument case. Tip: There are locking tuners with a built-in string cutter (e.g., Auto-Trim Tuning Machines).

Locking nut

On guitars with a double-locking tremolo (see page 69), you need to tighten the locking nut once you've brought the strings to pitch. Once the nut has been locked, you can tune the strings with the fine-tuning machines at the bridge only. If you open the locking nut to use the regular tuning machines, you risk breaking the strings where they run under the lock.

Stabilizing strings

New strings tend to detune quickly: They need to stabilize. To speed up this process, gently 'stretch' each string by sliding a finger under it and pulling it up. Then bring it back to pitch. Repeat this once or twice for all strings until their pitches don't change anymore.

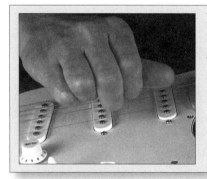

Tipcode EGTR-010
If you gently stretch your new strings, detuning will be reduced.

Gently press new strings down near the bridge.

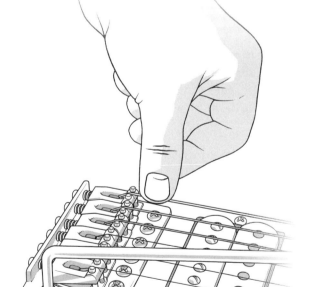

115

Near the bridge

New strings can also detune because they are not yet seated correctly at the bridge saddles. You help them do so by gently pressing them down right next to the saddles.

String tips

Here are some final string tips:

- If your instrument has **string trees**, you should use them.

- Prevent getting **kinks** in your strings when installing them; kinks can cause bad intonation and even breakage.

- Avoid **mixing up strings**: Don't unpack a string until you're ready to put it on. Companies that don't package their strings individually attach labels to them.

- **Tuning too high** can damage your strings or your instrument. Refer to Chapter 8 for more information.

- To improve tuning stability, some players apply a tiny drop of **Teflon lubricant** in the slots of the nut. You can also do so on the saddles and the strings' entries in the trem block.

- If you decide to remove all the strings from a **hollow-body guitar**, make sure that you know how (and where!) to replace the bridge. Also, put a cloth under the tailpiece to prevent it from damaging the finish when it comes loose.

8

Accessories

The main accessories for guitarists and bassists are cables, instrument cases or gig bags, straps, instrument stands, and picks. Here are their key details, and lots of helpful tips.

As long as you're still practicing at home, there's no reason to spend a lot of money on an instrument cable. When you start gigging, however, things change.

Long cables

The better your equipment — and your ears — the more important the quality of the cable will be, especially if you use one over fifteen feet long. The longer a cable gets, the more your clarity, definition, and dynamic range may suffer, unless you have an instrument with active electronics (see page 81–83). Spiral cables should usually be avoided.

Improve your sound

Expensive cables are typically more robust and therefore more reliable, with thoroughly attached plugs and well-protected cable ends. Good internal shielding reduces the chance of microphonic noise, hum, and interference. Better cables can make for a better sound too. Provided the rest of your equipment is good enough, they can help enhance clarity, definition, high frequency response, and even gain.

TIP

Question

Some experts seriously question whether cables have any significant effect on the sound, though, while others even claim to hear the subtle differences between the plugs of different brands.

Oxygen-free

Most cables use oxygen-free copper wire, which is said to help prevent corrosion and signal distortion.

Jacket

The ruggedness of the cable is in part determined by the material of the jacket. A good cable should also lay flat, with little or no 'memory,' and it shouldn't tangle or curl. Most cables have a synthetic jacket; others come with braided (woven) exteriors. Both types are available in a wide range of colors and designs, usually with a choice of straight and right-angle plugs.

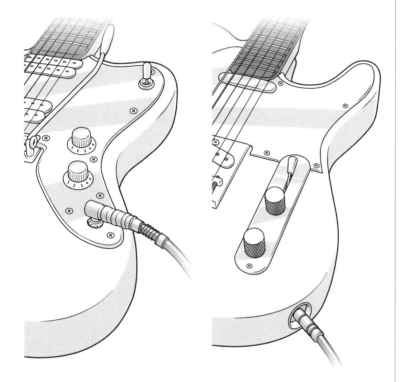

A right-angle plug (left) and a straight one (right).

Silent plugs

Some cables have special 'Silent' plugs or plugs with a built-in mute switch that prevent loud pops when unplugging your instrument. There are companies that make retrofittable cable accessories to the same effect.

Wireless

If you want to really move around onstage, you can consider a wireless system. A transmitter with an antenna is plugged into your instrument's output jack, and the receiver plugs into your amp or effects unit. Prices range from one hundred to six hundred dollars and more.

119

More?
There's much more on cables, plugs, and wireless systems in
Tipbook Amplifiers and Effects (see page 246).

CASES AND BAGS

Cases and gig bags offer protection against damage on the road,
but they're also useful in keeping airborne dust and dirt from your
instrument when you don't play.

Gig bags
Basic *gig bags* are available for as little as twenty dollars or less,
while leather models may cost as much as three hundred. More
money buys you a more effective (not necessarily meaning
thicker!) shock-absorbent padding, a tougher, water resistant
exterior, reliable zippers that won't scratch your instrument, and
wider, more comfortable adjustable shoulder straps and backpack
straps. Some bags (and cases) offer extra support and stabilization
for the – vulnerable – neck of the instrument.

Extra pockets
Most gig bags have extra pockets for spare strings, picks, an
electronic tuner, cables, sheet music, or even an instrument stand
or a music stand. Gig bags are less expensive, lighter, and easier

Gig bag.

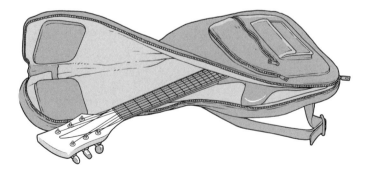

120

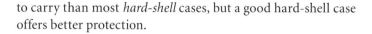

to carry than most *hard-shell* cases, but a good hard-shell case offers better protection.

Hard-shell cases
Cases come in different qualities too, starting at as little as forty dollars for a case with a chipboard shell. Cases with plywood or molded plastic shells are stronger, but more expensive. A hard-shell case needs to perfectly fit your instrument. For example, some designs fit both instruments with and without tilted headstocks (see page 54); others don't. Top quality cases may cost some four hundred dollars.

Form-fitting or rectangular
Form-fitting cases usually offer less room for accessories than rectangular models, but most have at least one padded accessory compartment. The instrument is protected against scratches by a soft (usually plush or plush cotton) lining. Some cases have special features such as a support channel for the neck, or a built-in hygrometer and humidifier, which can be important for hollow-body instruments. Well-designed models have one or more thoroughly attached handles at strategic places.

TIP

Remove your strap
Always remove the strap from your instrument before putting it in its case or bag. One of the reasons to do so is that some types of strap material may damage your finish.

GUITAR STANDS

Intermission? Put your instrument in a good stand, rather than leaning it against a wall, your amp, or a piece of furniture.

Small or big
Some stands have been designed to fit a large accessory pocket, when folded up. Others don't fold up that compactly, but are

121

designed for maximum stability. If you use more than one instrument, you can get yourself a multi-guitar stand; some cases even double as one.

Foldable guitar stand.

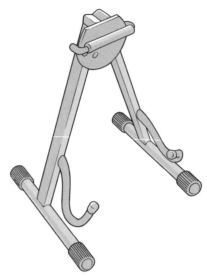

Cover the cushions
The padded arms and back rest of a guitar stand can damage some natural types of finish (e.g., nitro-cellulose). To prevent this, simply cover the pads with cotton cloth.

Neck support
Not all stands offer a separate neck support. The ones that do may have a security strap or a locking system for extra safety. On some stands, the neck support locks automatically (e.g., Auto Grab)

U-shape
Another product that helps prevent your guitar from falling over is a U-shaped plastic device that can plugged into a spare input or the headphone jack of your amp. There are similar products that can be stuck to a chair, an amp or a table, for instance.

Kickstand
The Kickstand is a very special type of guitar stand: It attaches to your instrument via the strap button. When not in use, you simply fold it against the back of your (bass) guitar.

122

STRAPS

Guitar straps are available in numerous designs and materials, from basic five-dollar synthetic straps to padded, genuine (suede, blasted, stonewashed, etc.) leather models that cost ten times as much.

Quick release
Commonly, the instrument's strap buttons need to be pushed through the slits in the strap ends. To save time and to prevent the slits from wearing out, some straps have a quick-release system that leaves the strap ends attached to the instrument.

Security lock system with special strap buttons and retainers (Schaller).

Locking the strap
More advanced designs feature a positive, spring-loaded locking system. They require that the regular strap buttons are replaced by special strap buttons; the strap gets matching strap retainers

123

at either end. These systems can be used on any guitar, with any standard strap. Installing them is a cinch.

TIP

> ### Flush buttons
>
> *If you don't like the sight of strap buttons, you can have countersunk flush 'buttons' installed. Only a few companies provide these inset receivers and matching retainers as a standard item.*

PICKS

Picks or *plectrums* come in numerous thicknesses, colors, shapes, sizes, and materials.

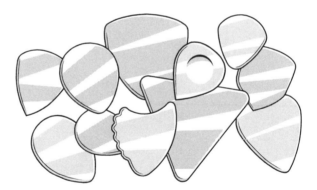

Light or heavy
Pick thicknesses typically range from about .020" to .125" (0.5–3.2 mm); some are even thicker.

- **Rhythm** guitar players tend to go for larger, softer, lighter-gauge picks which help produce bright, open sound.

- **Lead** players typically choose a thicker, harder type of pick, which allows them to play faster and more accurately. Harder picks also promote a heavier, fuller, stronger, and better defined tone.

124

Picks, fingers, and fingerpicks

Bassists who use a pick generally use special, large bass picks; most
bassist play with their fingers only, however. Some guitarists do
too, producing a very characteristic, warm, round type of sound.
Other players use finger picks, which are worn on individual
fingers.

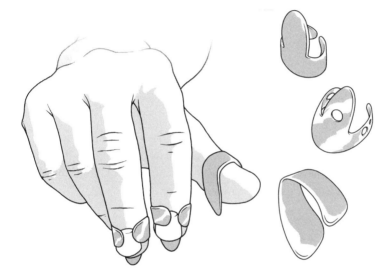

Fingerpicks

Materials

Most picks are synthetic. Celluloid is very popular, promoting a
warm, musical tone. It's not very durable, however, unlike acetal
polymer, a strong and resilient material generally known as Delrin.
To make them less slippery, Delrin picks often have a matte finish.
Other synthetics are used too, and so are wood, metal, horn, stone,
and felt, for a wide range of sounds and effects. Natural materials
are mainly used by hollow-body guitarists.

Anti-slip

Players with slippery fingers can choose from a wide variety of
slip-proof picks, ranging from models with cork patches, concave
knurled gripping areas, raised lettering, or a perforation.

Shape

How a pick plays and how it makes you sound also depends on

125

its shape. It can't hurt to experiment with pointed and rounded models.

TIP

Special picks

Besides the regular models, there are lots of variations on the theme, such as three-way picks (three picks of different gauges in one); picks with notched edges that create a grwwwww sound when slid across wound strings; and picks with a flexible 'hinge' in the middle.

Find the one you like

Most picks cost next to nothing. Experiment with different gauges and shapes until you find the one you like best. Cheap as they are, many picks have rough edges or other flaws. All it takes to finish them is a fine file or some fine sandpaper.

9

Tuning

Before you can start playing, you'll need to tune your instrument, or at least check whether it's still in tune. Tuning isn't that hard — though there's more to it than you may think. This chapter tells you the ins and outs of tuning with and without electronic tuners. Tuning tips for advanced players are included!

The notes that guitar and bass strings are usually tuned to, are shown on the keyboards below. Memory joggers for these notes are on pages 9–10.

Tuning a guitar to a piano.

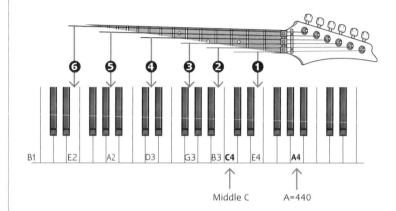

B1 E2 A2 D3 G3 B3 **C4** E4 **A4**

Middle C   A=440

Tuning a bass guitar to a piano.

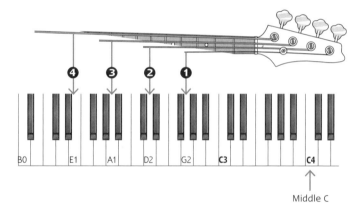

B0 E1 A1 D2 G2 **C3**   **C4**

Middle C

TIPCODE

Tipcode EGTR-011 and EGTR-012

These Tipcodes sound the reference pitches for guitar (Egtr-011) and bass guitar (Egtr-012). Low B is included for both instruments.

Extra strings

These diagrams also show the notes to which the extra string of a seven-string guitar is usually tuned (B1) and the extra strings of five-string (B0) and six-string basses (B0 and C3).

With and without tuners

Most guitarists and bassists tune their instrument with an electronic tuner, so that's where this chapter starts. As it's good to be able to check the tuning with your ears or to tune your instrument when your tuner breaks down, other tuning techniques are covered as well. Most players use a combination of these techniques.

Electronic tuners

To use an electronic tuner, you simply plug your instrument cable in its input, and play your first string. The tuner display will show you exactly whether the string is in tune, too high (*sharp*), or too low (*flat*).

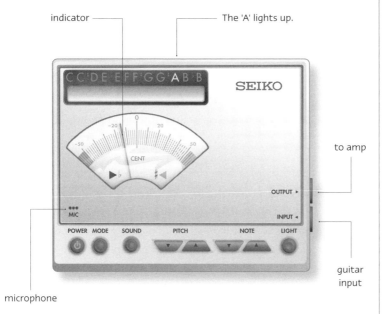

indicator — The 'A' lights up.

to amp

microphone

guitar input

An automatic, chromatic electronic tuner. The A it hears, sounds a little flat.

Basic

On the most basic type of tuner, you have to select the instrument you're going to tune (bass or guitar), and then the first string you will tune. Here is how these *manual tuners* work.

129

1. Select the instrument (check the tuner's manual).

2. Select low E.

3. Play low E, and don't play it too hard.

4. If the pointer shows that the string's pitch is too low, tighten the string a little. If it's too high, loosen it a bit.

5. When the pointer hits the middle of the scale, the string is in pitch.

6. Select the next string, tune it — and so on

7. When all strings have been tuned, check them once more, starting at low E.

Chromatic tuners

Most tuners are *chromatic tuners*, which automatically display which note they 'hear.' This type of tuner requires some very basic knowledge of music theory. If, for example, the tuner displays an F when you play the low E string, you need to know that this means that the string sounds a half step (or semitone) too high.

Faster

Assuming you do know all this, chromatic tuners work a lot faster. Also, they allow you to use open and other non-standard tunings (see page 141).

TIP

Numbered notes

Chromatic tuners often display numbered note names, as shown on the keyboard illustration above (e.g., E2 is the guitar's low E). Manual tuners often display the string numbers instead. In that case, that same low E is indicated as 6E, the sixth string of the instrument. Confusing, but true.

Use your ears

If you only use your eyes to tune your instrument, you won't train your ears to hear when a string goes out of tune. So it's good to listen to what you're doing. You can either connect the tuner's output to your amp, or plug your instrument directly into your amp and have the tuner's built-in microphone register the pitches you play. *Tip:* When tuning, turn your chorus and other (pitch modulation) effects off.

Tuners

Chromatic tuners are available from about twenty to one hundred dollars and more. For daily tuning purposes, a cheap one will do. If you also want to use it to adjust the intonation of your instrument, for example, you will want to get a better one that registers even the smallest pitch differences. Here are some other things to consider.

- Better tuners **respond faster** and may hold the reading a little longer.

- Better tuners offer a **wider tuning range**, up to seven octaves. Cheap tuners may not be able to accurately tune a five-string bass or a seven-string guitar, or register the high harmonics that are essential for adjusting the intonation of your instrument.

- Many good tuners also generate **reference pitches** (three or more octaves). The ones that do often have a separate headphone output.

- Also check how well the tuner can be read on a **dark stage** (some have a backlit display), and whether it shuts off automatically after a while, to save batteries.

- Tuners with a mechanical pointer are usually **slower** and use more energy than the ones with an LCD pointer. LED pointers (small 'lights') are easy to read on dark stages.

- Some tuners double as a **metronome** (see page 29).

- Some amplifiers and most multi-effects feature a **built-in tuner**!

- For onstage tuning, you may consider a **pedal tuner**. Make sure it has a true bypass (meaning that the guitar signal will not be affected by the tuner's electronics).

- Dedicated tuners also support **ultra-low tunings** used by heavy metal players, tuning up to five semitones below standard pitch.

131

Output

Most tuners have an output, allowing you to leave the tuner between your instrument and your amp or effects. However, most players prefer not to, unless the tuner features true bypass (meaning that the guitar signal will not be affected by the tuner's electronics).

A=440

If your guitar is in tune and you play the high E-string at the fifth fret, the string vibrates 440 times per second. This sounds the note A that most bands and orchestras tune to. It's known as A=440.

TIPCODE

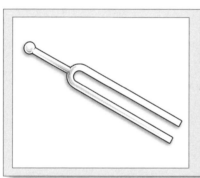

Tipcode EGTR-013
This Tipcode sounds A=440, the standard reference pitch produced by tuning forks (see page 134) and electronics metronomes.

Higher or lower

Some bands may want to tune slightly higher or lower, or you may have to adjust your tuning to a piano that has been tuned a bit too high or too low. For this purpose, good tuners can be calibrated to alternate pitches (e.g., from A=415 to A=450).

TIP

Onboard tuning

In 2008, N-Tune introduced an onboard tuner that can be installed into most electric guitars. Tuning the instrument is a matter of pulling the instrument's volume knob up, which activates the tuner. Once the guitar is tuned, you push the knob back down and play. There are also systems that tune your instrument for you, such as the German Powertune System, introduced in 2005.

132

Fifty cents

Many tuners indicate pitch deviations in cents, using a scale that runs from –50 to +50. Fifty cents equals a half step or semitone. Expensive models show deviations digitally in steps of one cent. This is very helpful for precise tuning and intonation.

STRING TO STRING

A traditional way to tune your instrument is to compare the pitches of fretted and open strings.

Low E and A

Provided low E is in tune, play this string at the fifth fret. Then compare the open A-string to it. Adjust the A-string until it sounds the same pitch.

Tipcode EGTR-014
This Tipcode shows you how to simply tune fretted to open strings on an acoustic guitar. It works just the same on an electric instrument.

TIPCODE

The other strings

When low A is in tune, play it at the fifth fret and adjust the open D-string to this pitch. Then tune the other strings according to the illustration on the next page.

Guitarists only

For guitarists only: Note that you stop the strings at the *fifth* fret each time, except when you tune open B. This string is tuned to the G-string played at the *fourth* fret.

133

IV, V

In diagrams that represent a guitar neck and strings, it's common to indicate the frets with Roman numerals: IV is the fourth fret, V is the fifth, and so on.

Tuning with fretted and open strings. Compare the two strings marked with the triangles below. The black dots indicate where to fret the strings. The open dots indicate the open strings. The resulting pitches are shown above the string names (EE, BB, etc.).

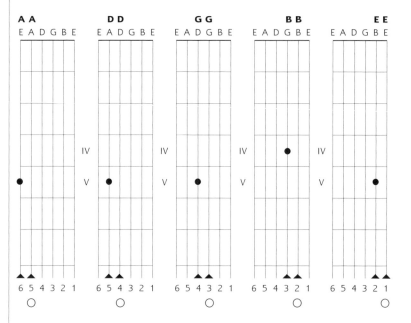

Bending strings

If you find it hard to hear whether a string sounds too high or too low, try bending the fretted string. This raises its pitch. If this makes it come closer to the open string's pitch, you need to tune the open string down, and vice versa.

Singing

You can also try to sing the notes you are comparing. You'll soon learn to 'feel' whether you need to sing higher or lower. Adjust the strings accordingly.

Tuning fork

If you don't have access to a tuner, a *tuning fork* will give you the reference pitch you need to tune reliably, by ear. You simply hit this low-cost, two-pronged fork on your knee, for example, and

134

then put the base of its stem on your instrument, or on a table top; this will enhance its volume. Electric guitarists generally don't use tuning forks, but it's good to know that they're around.

Tipcode EGTR-015
Tipcode Egtr-015 shows an A=440 tuning fork.

TIPCODE

Form in E

Most tuning forks produce the note A=440, because most musicians and bands tune to that note. For guitarists and bassists it's easier to get one that sounds an E, at the same pitch of the guitar's high E (329,6/330 Hertz). Tune this string to the fork, and then use the illustration on the previous page in reverse order: First tune the B-string at the fifth fret to high E, then tune G to B, and so on. Alternatively, you can tune low E to high E, and proceed from there.

Tuning fork in A

If you have a tuning fork in A, adjust the high E-string at the 5th fret to that pitch.

Too low or too high

If you play on your own, you don't need to tune to an exact reference pitch. If your instrument is tuned much too low, though, the low tension will make your strings buzz. If it's tuned way too high, your strings may break or you may damage your instrument.

TIP

135

Bass

To tune a bass to a tuning fork in A, play the G-string at the 14th fret. Your bass will then sound an A an octave below the pitch of the tuning fork.

HARMONICS

You can also compare string pitches using *harmonics* or *overtones*. This technique makes pitch differences a lot easier to hear.

Playing harmonics

It may take a little practice to play harmonics. Place a finger very lightly on the low E-string, barely touching it, exactly above the twelfth fret. Then strike the string. The thin, high tone you'll hear is a harmonic. You'll hear harmonics best when using the bridge pickup only.

Fifth, seventh, and so on

You can also play harmonics at other frets. For tuning, you use the fifth, seventh, and twelfth fret harmonics as follows:

Five and seven

Tune the strings to each other by comparing the fifth fret harmonic of each lower-sounding string to the seventh fret

TIPCODE

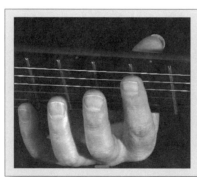

Tipcode EGTR-016
Tipcode Egtr-016 shows you how to tune using harmonics. On an electric guitar, preferably use the bridge pickup!

harmonic of the adjacent higher-sounding string. Start with E and A, and then move up.

High B and E
Tuning the B-string is different, again. Compare the seventh fret harmonic of low E to open B, or to its twelfth fret harmonic. Then tune high E: compare its seventh fret harmonic to the fifth fret harmonic on B. Finally, check your tuning. Also compare both E-strings, using harmonics on either both, or one of the strings.

B on the bass
To tune the low B-string on a bass, compare the seventh fret harmonic of low E to the twelfth fret harmonic of the B-string.

Keep on ringing
Using harmonics makes tuning easier because the notes are pure and the strings sustain longer.

Beats
Also, playing harmonics makes it easier to get two strings to sound at exactly the same pitch. Here's how: When the pitches you're comparing are very close, you will hear slower or faster 'waves.' These waves are known as *beats*. If you bring the two pitches even closer to each other, the beats will get slower. When they're gone, the two pitches are identical. If the beats get faster, you've gone too far, so back up and try again.

Tipcode EGTR-017
In this Tipcode, you can clearly hear how the number of beats is reduced as the strings are tuned up to the right pitch.

TIPCODE

137

Tuning fork in A

If you have a tuning fork in A, play the 5th fret harmonic on the A-string. When properly tuned, this will sound an A one octave below the tuning fork's A.

PROBLEM? SOLVED!

Unfortunately, the popular tuning method described above is not perfect. As you will hear — if you have a trained ear or good pitch — one or two of your strings may need additional tuning, depending on the chords you're playing. This has to do with the fact that this tuning method uses an interval called a *fifth* (the seventh fret harmonic sounds an octave and a fifth higher than the open string). In order to tune a guitar so that it always sounds in tune, fifths should be tuned a little flat. As this isn't that easy, it's better to go for a tuning method that does not include fifths. Here it is.

The solution

First tune your low E-string, using an electronic tuner.

1. Tune high E to the harmonic on the fifth fret of low E.

2. Tune your D-string: Play the twelfth fret harmonic on low E and compare this pitch to the E on the D-string in second position.

3. Tune your B-string: Play the B-string in third position and compare this pitch (D) to the twelfth fret harmonic on the D-string

4. Tune your G-string: Play the twelfth fret harmonic on the G-string and compare this pitch (G) to the G on high E in third position.

5. Tune your A-string: Play the twelfth fret harmonic on the A-string and compare this pitch to the A on the G-string in second position.

Now you guitar should sound in tune no matter which chord you're playing or which key you're in. As an alternative, there are

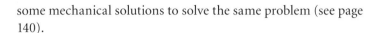

some mechanical solutions to solve the same problem (see page 140).

INTERVALS AND CHORDS

Advanced players often tune their instrument by listening to the pitch differences (*intervals*) between the strings, without fretting them or playing harmonics. The A-string is supposed to sound a perfect *fourth higher* than the low E-string.

Amazing Grace
A perfect fourth is the interval that you hear when you sing the first two syllables of *Amazing Grace* or *Here Comes the Bride*. Sing the first syllable of this song at the same pitch as your low E-string. Then tune the A-string to the pitch of the second syllable. The same interval is used when you go from strings A to D, D to G, and B to high E.

Oh When the Saints
The only interval that's different is the one from G to B. To tune the B-string to the G-string, sing the first two syllables of *Oh When the Saints Go Marching In*. This interval is called a *major third*.

Chords
Alternatively, you can check your guitar's tuning by playing chords and listening if they sound in tune. Preferably do this using one or more chords from the song you're about to play. However, you may find that while one chord sounds great, another one may sound completely off.

One sounds great — but the others
If you tune your guitar so that the first-position E-major chord sounds great, you'll find that that the first-position A-major chord sounds quite a bit less in tune (note the C♯ on the B-string!), and that D-major and C-major are even worse.

139

Solutions

The majority of players take these and other natural pitch deviations for granted. The ones that don't can choose from a variety of solutions, ranging from having the nut replaced and the intonation adjusted according to a special system (e.g., Buzz Feiten), to using two or more curved frets (e.g., Fretwave and True Temperament), or using special nuts (e.g., Earvana). As an alternative, you can use the tuning method described on page 138 (Problem? Solved!).

MORE TUNING TIPS

- Always **tune up** to the correct pitch. If a strings sounds too high, loosen it so it sounds too low and tune up from there. It's easier to hear what you're doing that way, and it helps improve tuning stability.

- You can tune your guitar or bass to a **pitch pipe**. Pitch pipes cost next to nothing, but they do go out of tune rather easily.

- You can also tune all your strings to the corresponding notes of a **keyboard instrument**.

- Do your strings go **out of tune quickly**, or is it hard to get them in tune? That could be the result of having too many windings around the tuning post (see page 114), worn strings, poor adjustment, too narrow nut slots, worn bridge saddles, a bad tremolo… Have your instrument checked by an expert, if you can't find the culprit(s!) yourself.

- Is tuning hard because the **strings stick in the slots** of the nut? This can be solved temporarily by frequently pressing the strings right behind the nut. Tune, press, listen, tune… Also try 'lubricating' the string slots by rubbing them with a soft lead pencil point. Ultimately, however, the nut should be replaced or adjusted.

- Does your guitar go out of tune after **severe string bends** or

140

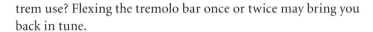
trem use? Flexing the tremolo bar once or twice may bring you back in tune.

- Do you have a tremolo bridge with fine-tuning machines (e.g., Floyd Rose)? Then **avoid leaning on the bridge** when tuning. Tune, let go of the fine-tuning machine, listen, tune again if necessary, and so on.

DIFFERENT TUNINGS

Some heavy metal players and other guitarists tune a half-step or more lower than the regular tuning. You can also *raise* the pitch of your strings, by using a capo (see page 142). Another tuning alternative is to use an open tuning.

Half-step, whole-step
Tuning a guitar lower than normal makes for a heavier, fatter, thicker sound. Also, the lower tension makes string bending easier. Combined with heavier-gauge strings, the sound becomes even punchier. Some players tune a half-step lower (E♭, A♭, D♭, G♭, B♭, E♭); others a whole step (D, G, C, F, A, D; sometimes referred to as a *D-neck*). On 7-string jazz guitars, low B is often tuned down to an A.

> #### Even lower
> If you tune a regular guitar even lower, you risk string buzz, except on guitars that are designed for such low tunings (page 165).

TIP

Adjustments
Using any of these lower drop tunings may require extra adjustments, as described in Chapter 10.

D-tuners and B-benders
For some songs, it can be useful to extend the range of your bass

or guitar to low D, which means tuning the low E-string a whole-step down. This drop-D tuning is easiest if your instrument has a *D-tuner*. A few instruments come with such a device; you can also have one retrofitted. A similar device, the *B-bender*, which raises the B a whole step (to C♯), is much rarer.

B to C

The lowest string on five- and six-string basses (low B) often sounds a bit weak, flabby, or indistinct. Some players make it sound punchier and tighter by tuning it a half-step up, from B to C.

A capo

For some songs, it can be easy to raise the pitch of your guitar entirely. You do so with a *capo*. This is a clamp that you simply attach at the required fret. If, for example, you want to raise the pitch a whole-step, you use it at the second fret, as shown below.

Always attach a capo close to the fret, where you would normally put your fingers. This type of capo can be mounted from the other side of the neck too (Shubb).

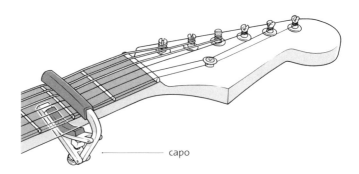

capo

Open tunings

Many players in a variety of styles use *open tunings*, meaning that the *open* strings are tuned to produce a certain chord. This allows you to play entire songs by simply putting a finger across all six strings (known as a *barre*), and sliding from chord to chord without using any difficult fingerings.

Two examples

Tuning your strings to D, G, D, G, B, and D (from thick to thin), for example, produces a G-major chord. Tuned to E, A, E, A, C♯, and E, the open strings ring an A-major chord.

142

10

Maintenance

Apart from cleaning, guitars and basses do not require a
lot of maintenance. There are some minor adjustments
you can easily do yourself. Other types of adjustment
are best left to an expert. This chapter ends with some
additional tips for taking your guitar on the road.

If you wipe your guitar — body, strings, neck — with a clean, soft, lint-free cloth each time you're done playing, it won't require much additional cleaning. When it does need extra attention, there are plenty of special cleaners to choose from.

Bodies and lacquered fingerboards
Most guitar and bass bodies have a polyurethane or nitrocellulose lacquer finish, which can be cleaned and restored to its original shine with most available guitar cleaners. The same goes for polyurethane lacquered fingerboards (i.e., most maple fingerboards).

Spray or cream
Some cleaners are a cream-like substance, others are sprays. Sprays are usually best for keeping relatively clean instruments clean, while cream cleaners are typically better suited for polishing the instrument — which indicates that they're (more or less) abrasive.

Which one?
Most cleaners can also be used to clean your instrument's hardware, knobs, and pickguard. Ask your dealer for advice, and try different cleaners to find which one works best for you. Always read the instructions first, and begin by trying a bit on a less visible section of your instrument.

TIP

Dust scratches
Use a soft brush or cloth to remove any dust before applying a cleaner. Dust scratches the instrument's finish, really!

Open pore
Special finishes may need special cleaners. Instruments with a wax or oil finish that leaves the pores of the wood open can usually be treated with the same substances that are used for non-lacquered fingerboards, such as lemon oil or fingerboard conditioner. Some experts advise beeswax. You can also try a mild guitar cleaner. If you're not sure what to use, ask your dealer for advice. Unfortunately, most companies do not include a cleaning manual with their instruments.

Don't

Experimenting with cleaners that weren't designed for musical instruments can damage your (bass) guitar. On the other hand, you should know that many players and technicians use furniture cleaners or automotive polishes with great results, and at a low price. Ask around!

The knobs

If the body needs to be cleaned thoroughly, it's good to remove not only the strings, but the knobs too. Some knobs have a small screw that you should loosen first; others are clamped on a split shaft. If you can't pull them off with your fingers, you may try using a screwdriver to push them upward, bit by bit, using a piece of cardboard to protect the body — but it's usually safer to have your technician do it.

TIP

Custom knobs

Now that you've removed your knobs, it might be good to know that custom knobs are available: You can replace the original items by skull-shaped or UFO-shaped knobs, for example. The same companies typically also offer pickguards and other guitar parts in a wide variety of designs.

Non-lacquered fingerboards

When you can clearly see your finger marks on a non-lacquered fingerboard, you're late cleaning it. Use a special fingerboard conditioner or lemon oil. Apart from cleaning the fingerboard, this also replenishes the oils in the wood and prevents it from drying out.

Do take all the strings off before treating the fingerboard, as strings and oil don't match, and again, read the instructions before using any type of cleaner or oil.

The frets

Clean, polished frets make playing easier. Various companies sell fret polishing cloths or (reusable) fret polishing paper.

145

Brands

Guitar cleaners and other maintenance products are supplied by companies like D'Andrea, Dunlop, Number One, GHS, and Kyser, and some guitar manufacturers have their own cleaners.

Cloths, brushes, and Q-tips

Apart from a few lint-free cloths (one to apply each type of cleaner or oil, another one to rub or buff), you can use a soft toothbrush, a paintbrush, or Q-Tips to get into the nooks and crannies of your instrument.

Scratchy controls

To clean scratchy controls, you need to expose the actual potentiometers or pots before you can treat them with contact spray. This spray is available in most hardware stores. If you're not absolutely sure of how to handle this, have your dealer clean the pots for you (and ask him to include the pickup selector).

ADJUSTMENTS

A well-adjusted guitar or bass is easier to play and easier to tune, and it sounds better too. This section covers the main adjustment jobs, including action or string height, the neck, tremolo, intonation, pickup height, and the stopbar tailpiece. Some of these adjustments require more experience and skill than you may think, so don't do anything yourself unless you're absolutely sure you can handle it.

STRING HEIGHT

The *string height* of a (bass) guitar is the distance between the strings and the frets, measured at the 12th fret. String height is often referred to as the *string action* or, briefly, *action*. However,

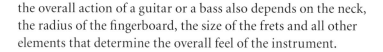

the overall action of a guitar or a bass also depends on the neck, the radius of the fingerboard, the size of the frets and all other elements that determine the overall feel of the instrument.

Low or high

If you go for speed and easy playability, you'll probably prefer a relatively low 'action.' A higher action makes playing a bit heavier, but it helps produce a stronger and fuller tone, crisper definition, more sustain, and cleaner, buzz-free chords, especially if you hit the strings hard. For bassists, slapping is easier with a relatively low action. If you go for extra volume and a large dynamic range, you may try setting your strings a bit higher.

Too high

If you feel you have to press the strings down real hard, string action may be too high. A very high string action will also cause intonation problems: pressing the string so far down raises its tension considerably, making the pitch go up too far.

Too low

If the strings are too low, they will rattle against the frets (fret buzz of string buzz), or they may choke when you bend them. Also, the string above the one you're bending may creep under your fingers and kill the tone.

Different strings

Other than changing string height because of the reasons mentioned above, adjustment may be necessary when you switch to heavier- or lighter-gauge strings (heavier strings raise the action; lighter-gauge strings lower the action), when you move from an environment with a relatively low or high air humidity, or when the seasons change: dry winter air can make the wood of your instrument contract so that string height increases, making for a stiffer string action — and vice versa.

Saddles, nut, and neck

String height can be adjusted by lowering or raising the saddle(s) or the nut, by adjusting the neck with the built-in truss rod, or by any combination of these three. Deciding what needs to be done

147

requires an expert eye. For example, raising the string height by adjusting the bridge saddles may have no use if the nut or the neck adjustment does not suit the string height you have in mind.

String height

As a starting point, high E should be at least 0.05" (³⁄₆₄" or 1.2 mm) above the 12th fret, and low E about 0.08" (⁵⁄₆₄" or 2 mm).

Bass guitars

Bass guitar strings need more room to move, of course, up to some 0.110" (⁷⁄₆₄" or 2.8 mm) for low E.

Drill bits

Measuring your instrument's exact string height can be awkward — but there's a simple solution: use drill bits of the correct size. Carefully stick them between the relevant fret and string.

Saddles

Most guitars and basses have individually adjustable saddles (one per string); some have one saddle per two strings; others have a

Section of a bridge with individually adjustable saddles.

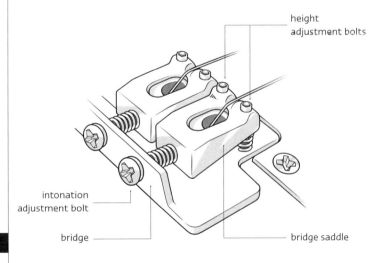

height adjustment bolts

intonation adjustment bolt

bridge

bridge saddle

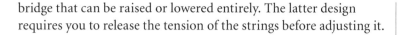

bridge that can be raised or lowered entirely. The latter design requires you to release the tension of the strings before adjusting it.

Truss rod or nut

Adjusting string height with the saddles is basically a matter of fine-tuning. For larger changes, you typically need to have the nut replaced or the truss-rod adjusted — which is best left to a technician.

The neck

The neck and fingerboard should be very slightly concave along their length, dipping a little between headstock and body. This so-called *neck relief* helps prevent string buzz or fret buzz.

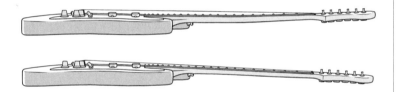

The neck of the upper guitar is way too concave; the other is convex.

Check

You can check the neck relief by fretting low E at both the 1st and the 15th frets. (Using a capo at the 1st fret makes this a lot easier.) When held down at these two points, there should be a small gap between the string and the middle frets. If there isn't, your neck is either flat or convex, and strings may buzz. If the gap is larger than about 0.040" (1 mm), the instrument will be quite hard to play. In both cases, the neck should be adjusted with its truss rod. Again, this is best left to a technician.

(Don't) do it yourself

If you want to try adjusting the truss rod yourself, please note that minor adjustments often will do (think an 1/8 of a turn, maximum, to avoid damaging the instrument). Loosening the rod will lower string height, and vice versa. Tip: try out truss rod adjustments on an affordable instrument, rather than on a collector's item.

149

TIP

S-necks and kinks

Some necks have a slight S-shape, being concave up to the 8th fret, and then convex; others have a kink in the 13th/15th fret area, which can result in choking strings when bending them at those and higher frets. Both problems require expert help.

TREMOLO

Tremolo adjustment is adjusting the balance between the strings that pull on one side, and the tremolo springs that pull on the other. This is critically important for both the playability and the sound of your instrument. Switching to lighter or heavier strings usually requires adjusting the tremolo, and it even may need to be adjusted when switching from one string brand to another.

Tremolo springs should be well-adjusted too.

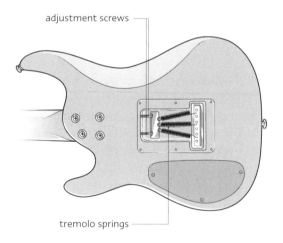

adjustment screws

tremolo springs

INTONATION

150

On most instruments, the bridge saddles can be adjusted lengthwise. This adjustment, the *intonation*, is important for how

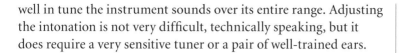

well in tune the instrument sounds over its entire range. Adjusting the intonation is not very difficult, technically speaking, but it does require a very sensitive tuner or a pair of well-trained ears.

Moving the saddles

You set the intonation by moving the saddles forward or backward. On some bridges this is easier than on others.

The twelfth harmonic, the twelfth fret

The most basic and best-known way to set the intonation is to adjust each string so the pitch of its twelfth fret harmonic is identical to the pitch when you fret the string at that point.

1. Tune your instrument.

2. Play the twelfth fret harmonic of the low E (see page 136).

3. Play the low E at the twelfth fret.

4. Compare the two pitches.

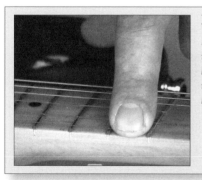

Tipcode EGTR-018
Play this Tipcode to see how to compare the pitches of the harmonic and the fretted note at the twelfth fret, and to hear how big that pitch difference can be.

TIPCODE

Higher or lower

If the fretted note sounds higher than the harmonic, the distance between the fret and the saddle is too short. The solution is to move the saddle backward, away from the fret. If the fretted note sounds lower, you need to move the saddle forward, toward the pickups.

Move, tune, compare

Moving the saddle forward or backward, even ever so slightly, will

151

make the pitch drop or rise considerably. Make sure you tune the string to its proper pitch before comparing the harmonic and the fretted note again. When the first string is okay, proceed with the other strings.

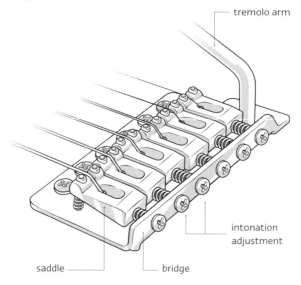

tremolo arm

intonation adjustment

saddle ——————— bridge

TIPCODE

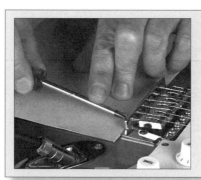

Tipcode EGTR-019
Moving the saddle toward the pickups lowers the pitch of the open string.

Tips

- Put your instrument flat on a table, and **protect both** by using a towel or a piece of foam plastic underneath. Support the neck in a similar way.

- Use a piece of **cardboard** to prevent your tools from scratching the body.

152

- When comparing the pitches, try not to vary **the way you pluck and fret** the strings.

- To prevent the strings from binding at the nut or the saddles, **stretch** them every time you've moved the saddle.

- The intonation can be set properly only when your strings are in prime condition: clean, and **preferably new.**

- Make it a habit to **check and adjust** your intonation after every string change.

- Note that it's **close to impossible** to get a string to sound exactly the same pitch when comparing the fretted note and the harmonic at that fret — but you can get close.

- You can also **check intonation** by comparing the open string to the twelfth harmonic of each string!

Another one

A more advanced way to adjust intonation is to go from string to string. Here's how:

1. The fifth fret harmonic of low E should produce the same pitch as the A-string played at the nineteenth fret. Adjust the A-string saddle to match the harmonic. Proceed likewise with the other strings (except for the B-string, which should be played at the twentieth fret).

2. Then compare the seventh fret harmonic of low E to the A-string's fourteenth fretted note. You will probably find that the fretted note is a bit flat. If so, raise it ever so slightly by adjusting the corresponding saddle. Adjust the other strings likewise (except for the B-string, which should be played at the fifteenth fret).

3. Finally, adjust the low-E saddle by comparing the twelfth fret harmonic on the A-string to low E's seventeenth fretted note.

Not so easy

Not all bridge designs allow for an easy adjustment of the intonation. Ask your dealer for advice. Properly adjusting a one-piece, floating bridge is an expert's job.

153

PICKUP HEIGHT

Pickup height can be adjusted, sometimes even per string. If a pickup is set too low, you will have low output, and your dynamic range and brightness will suffer. If you move it closer to the strings, attack and output will increase, but the tone may become harsh and edgy. What's worse, the magnet(s) may keep the strings from vibrating properly. This is commonly known as *string pull*.

Extreme
In the extreme case (strong magnet, close to the strings), string pull can make strings clatter against the fingerboard. In a milder case, string pull may produce false overtones or harmonics.

Warble
The mildest form of string pull adds a very slight 'warble' to the tone, a bit like what a *chorus* does. Some guitarists find this an indispensable element of their tone.

Do it yourself
Adjusting pickup height is quite easy, though it may take you quite some trial and error to find the sweet spots for your two or three pickups.

The right height
Most players will try to find the height that gives them maximum output without string pull. Some like to set the bridge pickup very high for solos, and the neck pickup pretty low for chord playing; you can also try setting different heights on the treble and bass sides.

TIP

Thumb rest
Bass players often use one of their pickups as a thumb rest. For that purpose, you should be able to secure this pickup in both high and low positions.

OTHER ADJUSTMENTS

If your guitar has a stopbar tailpiece, you can raise it to reduce the pressure of the strings on the bridge saddles. This makes for a 'singing' timbre with additional overtones. Lowering the stopbar increases the string pressure. This promotes a tighter, brighter, punchier sound, with more attack. However, the reduced angle at the bridge also increases the risk of breaking strings.

INTERFERENCE

Almost all guitars and bass guitars buzz, hum, or hiss to some extent. If there's too much noise, the culprit may be your cable, your instrument, your amp, or fluorescent lighting, a main outlet, a nearby railroad line, the stage lighting — you name it.

Cable, instrument, amp?
The easiest way to check the cable is by replacing it with your backup cable. Likewise, you can check your instrument by replacing it with another bass or guitar, using the same amp and cable.

The instrument
A noisy instrument can be the result of bad connections, a worn output jack, or lack of shielding. Both the cable and your instrument should be shielded, the latter by using grounded metal foil or conductive paint in the body cavities. Three tips:

• Humbucking pickups are **less noisy** than single-coil pickups.

• **Active pickups** are even quieter.

• **Distortion effects** amplify everything, noise included.

Plugs and noise suppressors
If the interference is not in your equipment, you can try using

155

another outlet, or putting the plug in the other way around (if the type of plug in your country allows for that). If you're near a power station, a railroad, or other high-voltage cables, then special noise suppression equipment may be required.

ON THE ROAD

Planning to go out with your instrument? Then first read this:

- Make sure you bring along spare **strings, picks,** and a **cable.** Don't forget spare batteries for instruments with active electronics, and for effects and tuners.

- Never leave your equipment in a car unattended.

- In a car, the best place for your instrument is usually on the floor **between the back and front seats**.

- Wooden instruments don't like sudden **changes in temperature and humidity**. If it's cold outside, it's best to allow your instrument to adjust to room temperature by leaving it in its case for a while. Hollow-body instruments are more vulnerable than solidbodies, in every respect.

- Never leave your instrument where it can get **too hot**.

- **Extremely dry air** (e.g., wintertime, air conditioning, central heating) can make the action go up and — eventually — your instrument crack. The best humidity level, both for instruments and people, is about 40 to 60%.

- Flying? Then it's best to carry your instrument as **carry-on luggage**, if that's allowed.

- If your guitar has a **serial number**, you'll probably find it on the back of the head, or on the label, or somewhere else inside the body. Jot it down, preferably before your instrument is stolen or lost. There's room to do so on page 240.

- Consider **insuring your instrument**, especially if you're taking it on the road, which includes visiting your teacher. Musical instruments fall under the 'valuables' insurance category. A regular homeowner insurance policy will not cover all possible damage, whether it occurs at home, on the road, in the studio, or onstage.

11

History

The solid-body guitar and bass have only been around since the 1950s, playing a leading role in a wide variety of musical styles ever since.

Even though they are different in many ways, the electric guitar clearly stems from its acoustic namesake. The history of the acoustic guitar starts thousands of years ago, when supper was still something you hunted for. Humans soon discovered that shooting an arrow produces a tone, due to the vibration of the string. Many years later, someone found a way to amplify that sound by attaching a gourd to the bow. That was the first forefather of the guitar.

Seventeenth century guitar with five pairs of strings.

Luthier
Numerous variations on the very first string instruments have appeared all around the world, eventually leading to the modern-day guitar. One of its best-known ancestors is the medieval lute, which explains why guitar makers are still referred to as *luthiers*. The first instruments resembling today's acoustic guitar emerged in the sixteenth century. These guitars often had five single or double strings, lacking a low E.

The classical guitar
Around 1850, the Spanish luthier Antonio de Torres combined a slightly bigger soundbox with an improved bracing pattern (*fan-bracing*) and a new scale, creating the guitar on which all modern classical, nylon-string guitars are based.

The steel-string guitar
Around the same time, the American guitar maker George Friedrich Martin designed the forerunner of today's steel-string acoustic guitar. This instrument had a larger soundbox than the nylon-string guitar, and a special bracing system (*X-bracing*).

160

Frying pan
The instrument that is considered to be the first electric guitar was built in the early 1930s by George D. Beauchamp. This 'Frying Pan' was made for Adolph Rickenbacker.

Les Paul and Paul Bigsby
Some ten years later, guitarist Les Paul made one of the earliest solid-body guitars by modifying an Epiphone guitar. The guitar that Paul Bigsby helped create around 1947 was another step closer to the modern solid-body. In 1948, Gibson made the first guitars with two pickups, allowing for previously unknown tonal variations.

Fender Broadcaster
In 1950, Fender introduced the world's first mass-produced solid-body electric. This Leo Fender design, first called Broadcaster and then renamed Telecaster, is available to this day.

Strat
The best-known electric guitar design is Fender's Stratocaster, introduced in 1954. Many, many guitars have been based on this instrument, which is still available in many different versions and price ranges.

Again: Les Paul
Shortly later, Gibson introduced the humbucking pickup. This soon became the standard pickup on the famous Gibson Les Paul guitars (1952), another design that never left the scene.

Bass guitars
After Leo Fender built his first solid-body guitars, he realized he could make bass guitars the same way. This would free the double-bassist from the huge 'doghouse' and provide loads of extra volume too.

Precise
Double basses don't have frets, but Fender used frets on their first electric bass guitars. The name of these basses, Precision, refers to the 'precise' intonation of a fretted instrument.

161

Then and now

Most of today's electric guitars and basses are largely based on the original designs mentioned above — and many players would love to have and play an instrument from that era. On the other hand, the guitar industry has come up with numerous inventions, improvements, and alterations: active electronics, noiseless pickups, graphite reinforcements, dual truss rods, new body and neck materials, headless body designs, locking tremolos, flush strap locks, locking tuning machines, coated strings, D-tuners, guitar synthesizers, and so on. And of course, the solid-body concept has always allowed for the wildest body designs. This started as early as in 1958, when Gibson introduced its Flying V, another classic instrument that has been around for decades.

*A Gibson
Flying V from
1958.*

12

The Family

Electric guitars and basses belong to the family of string instruments. Within that family they're usually referred to as fretted instruments, contrary to violins and cellos, for example. This chapter covers just a few of the many different guitars and basses, both electric and acoustic, as well as some other fretted relatives.

There are basses with rubber strings, electric travel guitars with a collapsible 'body' and a headphone output, basses with violin-like bodies, guitars with touch-sensitive sensors rather than strings, and instruments with five necks — but they're rare. Much more common variations include double-neck instruments, multi-string models, headless designs, and guitars and basses with nonstandard scales.

Violin bass (Höfner).

Double-necks
Double-neck instruments come in various configurations: a six-string and a twelve-string guitar neck, for example; or a six-string fretted and a four-string fretless bass neck; or a six-string electric and a six-string acoustic instrument.

A Gibson Double-Neck: One neck has six strings, the other twelve.

More strings
Though they're less common than acoustic twelve-string guitars, electric twelve-string instruments are available. So are ten-string models, on which the four top strings are doubled to produce a richer, fuller sound.

164

Multi-string basses

Since the 1980s, five-string basses have become increasingly popular, and there are plenty of six-string models around too. Some companies also built basses with even more strings (seven, eight, nine…). Other designs feature a combination of bass and guitar strings. One example is an eight-string instrument with a guitar string next to each bass string (tuned an octave apart). This makes each note sound as if it's played simultaneously on a bass and a guitar. More than a dozen companies make twelve-string basses, with two extra guitar strings for each bass string. If you feel that less is more, you can also get yourself a three-string bass (typically tuned to E, A, D, as played by Tony Levin and others).

A twelve-string bass guitar (Hamer).

Lower tunings

To allow for really low guitar tunings without fret buzz, a few companies make instruments with extra long scales. Some call them *baritone guitars*; other names refer to the 'subsonic' character of the instruments, or to the lowered 'drop' tuning. Scale lengths vary from a little under 27" to over 30". It is typically tuned a fourth below a regular guitar (i.e., B, E, A, D, F♯, B).

Higher tunings

Conversely, some bass guitars have been designed for higher tunings. Two examples are the *piccolo bass*, usually tuned to the same notes as the four lowest-sounding guitar strings, and the *tenor bass*, tuned to A, D, G, C (a fourth above a regular bass).

Headless

In the early 1980s, Ned Steinberger developed a bass guitar which had the tuning machines at the tail, making the headstock redundant. This design paved the way for more headless instruments, both basses and guitars. Instead of wood, Steinberger used a reinforced glass and carbon fiber resin.

Headless bass guitar (Steinberger).

Upright electrics

The electric bass guitar is of course directly related to the double bass — which, at the same time, is a completely different instrument. A few companies produce a cross between the two. These electric upright basses combine the playing position, the long neck, and the fretless fingerboard of a double bass, with the pickup and the solid or chambered body of an electric bass guitar.

TIPCODE

Tipcode EGTR-020
Play this Tipcode to hear what a double bass sounds like.

ACOUSTIC GUITARS

Acoustic guitars are designed to be played acoustically: without an amplifier, that is. The soundbox amplifies the sound of the strings.

Classical, nylon strings

The classical, nylon-string, or 'Spanish' guitar is used mainly but not exclusively for classical music. The nylon strings (three wound, three plain) make for a warm, colorful sound. There is little or no variation in body size, scale, or other dimensions, apart from some special designs and down-sized models for children.

Tipcode EGTR-021
This Tipcode demonstrates the sounding difference between a classical guitar and a steelstring.

  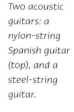
TIPCODE

Two acoustic guitars: a nylon-string Spanish guitar (top), and a steel-string guitar.

Steel-string guitars

The steel-string guitar, an American invention, typically has a larger soundbox than the classical guitar, but there are models with small bodies too. To distinguish them from acoustic guitars with an arched top, these acoustic steel-string instruments are also known as flat-top guitars.

ACOUSTIC-ELECTRIC (BASS) GUITARS

To allow acoustic guitars and bass guitars to be used on larger stages and in electric bands, many of them have a pickup, usually hidden under the saddle. These instruments are commonly known as acoustic-electrics (or electro-acoustics, etc.).

Piezo pickups

Most acoustic-electric guitars and basses use a *piezo* or *piezo-electric pickup*. These pressure-sensitive pickups respond to the pressure variations caused by the vibrations of the strings, and convert them to electric signals. Contrary to magnetic pickups, piezo pickups work with both nylon and steel-strings. Their relatively weak signal is boosted by a small preamp that is built

Control panel on an electro-acoustic guitar.

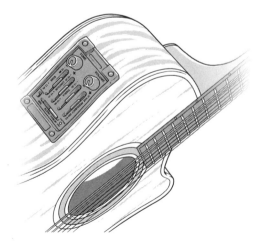

168

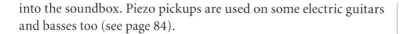

into the soundbox. Piezo pickups are used on some electric guitars and basses too (see page 84).

Controls

Volume and tone controls are usually located in a control panel on the instrument's left upper bout, or in the soundhole. Some of these systems also feature built-in effects, or a tuner.

Acoustic or electric?

Many guitars are neither fully electric nor completely acoustic. An example would be the type of 'classic electric' guitar with a shallow, almost solid body (sometimes referred to as a *semi-solid*) and a piezo pickup; or an instrument that plays like an electric guitar yet has a very acoustic sound; or an acoustic-electric with a rather shallow body in the shape of a well-known solid-body. The names of such guitars often indicate what they're about: Classic Electric (Gibson), Acousticaster (Godin), Stratacoustic (Fender), and Ampli-Coustic (Renaissance) are just some examples.

Tipbook Acoustic Guitar

More information about acoustic and acoustic-electric guitars can be found in *Tipbook Acoustic Guitar*.

MORE FRETTED INSTRUMENTS

Guitars and bass guitars are not the only fretted instruments. A brief look at the banjo, the mandolin, the saz, and other examples.

Lute

The lute is the ancestor of the acoustic guitar, with a pear-shaped body, a rounded back, and sides made of wooden strips, a short, wide neck, wooden tuning pegs. Its intimate, mellow sound perfectly matches the music of its era.

Mandolin

The original mandolin, with an even shorter neck, is closely

169

related to the lute. Modern mandolins look quite different, as the illustration shows: They still have a short neck, but an arched top (though flat-top models are available too) and, often, a flat back. The four pairs of strings are tuned to G, D, A, and E, from high to low. The two G-strings have the same pitch as the guitar's G string. Some variations on the mandolin are the *mandola*, the twelve-string *mandriola*, and the *mandocello*.

Mandolin.

Banjo

The *banjo* has a round sound box and a drumhead instead of a wooden top. Its four or five steel-strings generate a very short,

A five-string banjo.

percussive sound. Five-string banjos, like the mandolin, are mainly used in bluegrass and country, while the four-string is often played in folk and Dixieland bands. Six-string instruments are also available.

Steel guitar

The electric steel guitar is played horizontally, strings facing up, either on the player's lap or mounted on a frame. The strings are played with one or more picks. A slide is used instead of fretting the strings. (There are no frets.) *Pedal steel guitars* feature a number of pedals and/or levers to change the tuning. The instrument often has more than one neck, with eight, ten or more strings per neck. Resonator guitars are also used as steel guitars, typically featuring a very high action and — often — a square neck.

Chapman Stick

The Chapman Stick, introduced in the mid-1970s, is an interesting cross between a guitar, a bass, and (perhaps) a piano. With eight to twelve strings that are tapped rather than plucked or strummed, the instrument allows you to simultaneously play a melody or a solo, a bass part and chords — just like a pianist. Other makers have more recently introduced similar instruments, some with even more strings.

Balalaika, saz, and bouzouki

Fretted instruments are used in many other cultures as well. The Russian *balalaika*, for example, with its large, triangular soundbox; or the Turkish *saz-baglama*, with adjustable(!) frets and a small, pear-shaped body; or the Greek four-course (eight strings in four pairs) *bouzouki*.

13

How They're Made

Guitars and basses are made both in fully-automated plants and hands-on small workshops, thousands per day, or one per month — but the basic principles of making a traditional, wood-bodied guitar or bass are essentially the same.

'Solid' guitar and bass bodies usually look like they're made of a single piece of wood, but that's rarely the case. Typically, a body consists of two or more blocks of wood, or it's laminated. Instruments with a transparent finish usually have a separate top ply as well.

Bookmatched

In the higher price ranges, two-piece bodies and guitar tops are often bookmatched: A single piece of wood is split so that it can be folded open like a book. Then, the halves (their grains showing a matching, mirror image) are glued together. As well as looking good, bookmatching makes the instrument highly resistant to warping.

Bookmatched solid-body.

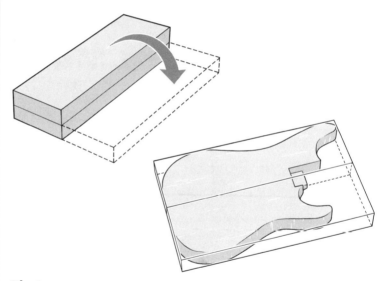

Photo

On less expensive instruments with a see-through finish, the top may look like (bookmatched) wood, but it's actually a photo, as described on page 43.

Handwork or machines

Shaping the body can involve anything from old-fashioned handwork to using advanced, computer-controlled machinery, such as CNC routing machines to cut the cavities for the pickups and potentiometers, as well as the pocket for the neck.

The neck

The neck, also, is often made of several pieces of wood, using similar wood-working machines. On through-neck instruments, the body consists of two 'wings' that are glued to the neck. Presses are used to properly seat the frets, which are mounted into carefully positioned slots.

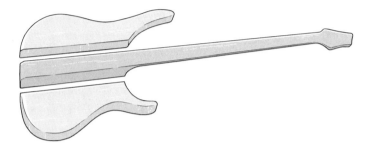

Through-neck.

Finishing

Finishing the body and the neck often involves applying various coats, each one preceded by carefully sanding the wood. At the end, most instruments are buffed to a high-gloss finish.

Assembly

Assembling the instrument includes gluing or screwing the neck onto the body, and installing the pickups and other electronic components, the hardware, and the strings. Most companies buy both their electronics and their hardware from other sources.

Do it yourself

As all components (necks, bodies, pickguards — you name it) are readily available, electric guitars are among the easiest instruments to make yourself. However, don't be disappointed if a homemade guitar costs more, and sounds and looks worse than one that you buy off the shelf.

Hollow-body instruments

Expensive hollow-body guitars have bookmatched tops and backs that are hand-carved in shape; a very time-consuming affair. The sides of the soundbox (the ribs) are made with the help of a mold. Thin linings help to hold the top, sides, and back together.

175

14

The Manufacturers

There are hundreds of guitar companies and individual guitar makers. This chapter introduces you to some of the main brand names you'll come across.

The guitar and bass market is quite confusing. Not only because there are so many brand names, but also because company A produces guitars for brands B and C, while brand B has another range of instruments made by company D...

One brand, several factories

Many guitar companies, both large and small, have their instruments made in various countries: their budget series in Asia, their intermediate instruments in the Czech Republic or Mexico, and their professional products in the US, for example.

One factory, several brands

Many — mainly Asian — manufacturers produce instruments and parts for several brands, one of them being their own 'house' brand. These companies, referred to as original equipment manufacturers (OEM), also supply dealers who sell instruments under their private brand names.

An indication

Some of the brands listed in this chapter can be found in pretty much every music store; others are less common. By the time you read these pages, certain companies may have disappeared; others may have been introduced; brand names may have been sold to other companies; and instrument makers may have added instruments in other prices ranges to their catalog(s). In other words, the following information is merely an indication of what's available, and it's by no means intended to be complete. Please refer to the specialized magazines and websites (see pages 192–194) for up-to-date information.

All price ranges

A few companies present instruments in pretty much all price ranges. These are the better-known names in the guitar industry. Most of them market acoustic guitars, amplifiers, effects, strings, and other musical products as well.

Fender and Squier

The American company **Fender** was the first manufacturer to produce solid-body guitars and basses. Their products are made in various countries, including the US, China, and Mexico. The **Squier** brand name, owned by Fender, is mainly used for lower-priced instruments. The Fender company owns a large number of guitar brands.

Gibson and Epiphone

Gibson, founded in 1902 by Orville Gibson, is another classic name. In the early 1930s, Gibson built its first semi-acoustic instrument, the Electric Spanish Guitar. The Gibson name is found on professional guitars only. Another complete line of instruments is marketed under the Epiphone name.

Japan

Two of the main Japanese brand names are **Ibanez** and **Yamaha**. Ibanez was originally a Spanish guitar distributed by Hoshino, a company that started selling sheet music in 1908. Some fifty years later, Hoshino introduced the first original Japanese electric Ibanez guitars. Yamaha started as a one-man organ factory in 1889 and evolved into the world's largest manufacturer of musical instruments.

American companies

Most other companies that market instruments in various price ranges are American by origin. Among them are **Dean**, **ESP, Fritsch, Hamer, Jackson, Peavey**, and **Washburn**. Their professional models are usually US-made; the less expensive instruments are often made overseas. **Harmony** (1892) at one time produced half of the US-made guitars each year. The company was reintroduced in 2008.

Starting low

Some examples of companies that focus on low-budget instruments are **Austin, AXL, Behringer, Daisy Rock, Danelectro, Encore, Jay Turser, Johnson, Lotus, Sunlite**, and **Rockwood**. Their price lists typically start around two hundred dollars or even lower.

A bit higher

Others start a bit higher, and often include intermediate — and sometimes professional — instruments too. Examples are **Aria**,

179

Aslin Dane, B.C. Rich, Cort, Fernandes, Hagstrom, Hohner, Lag, LTD (related to ESP), Samick, Schecter, and Tradition. Samick is one such manufacturer that builds instruments for various — Japanese, European, American — companies.

... and higher

Blade, Carvin, Chandler, Dean, Godin, Hallmark, Maverick, Schecter, and Vintage are a few examples of brands that you'll mainly find higher up in the budget range, throughout the intermediate price range; some are represented in the professional range as well.

Professional only

The number of guitar brands that specialize in the professional price range (list prices starting around fourteen or fifteen hundred dollars) is endless. A few of the better-known names include Alembic, Baker, Brian Moore, Charvel, Framus, G&L, Gretsch, Modulus, Moonstone, Music Man, Paul Reed Smith, Rickenbacker, Sadowsky, Tom Anderson, Vigier, and Warrior. You could make a list of at least the same length mentioning names of hollow-body specialists, such as Benedetto, Höfner, Guild, Heritage, and Renaissance. Some companies at one point extend their range to include lower priced instruments as well, e.g.. Parker Guitars, Paul Reed Smith (with their entry level SE guitars) and Ken Smith Design basses.

Basses only

Most specialized bass companies focus on the professional range. A few include instruments in the lower or intermediate price range too. Three examples are MTD, Spector, and Warwick.

Custom-made

There are many individual guitar or bass manufacturers whose names are not included in this chapter. To locate them, consult the magazines and other resources listed on pages 192–194. Note that some of the companies mentioned above offer custom-made instruments as well, allowing customers to choose from numerous types of woods, finishes, pickup configurations, necks, and fingerboards.

Pickups and hardware

Many guitar makers, large and small, buy many of the
components they use from other companies, rather than making
them themselves. The same products are also often used to
upgrade or revamp instruments. Some of the better-known pickup
makers include **Joe Barden**, **Bartolini**, **EMG**, **Evans**, **DiMarzio**,
Lawrence, **Lindy Fralin**, and **Seymour Duncan**. Major names
in tuning machines and other hardware items include **Gotoh**,
Grover, **Hipshot**, **Kluson**, **Schaller**, and **Sperzel**.

Glossary

This glossary briefly explains all the jargon touched on so far. It also contains some terms that haven't been mentioned yet, but which you may come across in other books, in magazines, or online. Most terms are explained in more detail as they are introduced in this book. Please consult the index on pages 242–243.

Action
Often used to indicate string height, but the overall action of an instrument is also determined by the shape of the neck, the fingerboard radius, the frets, and other factors.

Active EQ
Extended tone control, mostly used on bass guitars.

Active pickups
Active pickups produce a clean, noise-free signal. Can be found on basses and guitars.

Adjustment
A well-adjusted guitar or bass sounds better and is easier to play.

Archtop
Instruments with an arched top; commonly used to indicate hollow-body instruments.

Binding
A decorative and protective strip, running along the edge of the body or neck.

Bookmatched
A bookmatched body or top is made from a single piece of wood which is split so that it can be folded open like a book.

Bout
The shoulders and hips of the body are also known as the upper and lower bout.

Bridge
The strings run from the tuning machines to the bridge which usually has individually adjustable bridge saddles to set string height and intonation.

Bridge pickup
The pickup closest to the bridge.

Bridge saddles
See: *Saddles.*

Coil
Most pickups have one or two coils, i.e., magnets with copper wire wound around them. See also: *Single-coil pickup* and *Humbucker.*

Coil-tap
A coil-tap allows you to make a humbucker behave like a single-coil pickup.

Compound-wound strings
Strings with several windings.

Cutaway
Recessed part of the body; provides easier access to the higher frets.

Double-locking tremolo
See: *Locking nut, Lock-nut.*

D-tuner
Device which allows you to quickly detune the low E-string to a D.

Dual-coil pickup
See: *Humbucker.*

ƒ-Hole guitar
Another name for arch-top guitar, which usually has two ƒ-shaped sound holes.

Fingerboard
When you play, you press the strings to the fingerboard. Also called fretboard.

Flat-wound strings
Strings wound with a flat ribbon, as opposed to roundwounds. See: *Round-wound strings*.

Floating
Hollow-bodies often have a floating tailpiece, bridge, and pickguard, and sometimes a floating pickup too, which allows the guitar's top to resonate freely.

Four-conductor wiring
Allows for alternative wiring combinations (e.g., series, parallel, split-coil) of a humbucker.

Fretboard
See: *Fingerboard*.

Frets
The metal strips on the fingerboard or fretboard.

Hard-tail guitar
See: *Tremolo*.

Hardware
The metal components of a guitar (bridge, tuning machines, etc.).

Hollow-body
An electric guitar with a soundbox or resonance chamber. See also: *Archtop* and *Solid-body*.

Humbucker
A dual-coil pickup, designed to

'buck the hum' often emitted by single-coil designs. Sounds thicker and warmer than a single-coil pickup.

Intonation
A guitar with proper intonation sounds in tune over the entire range of the fingerboard.

Locking nut, lock-nut
A clamp that fixes your strings at the nut; part of a locking tremolo. Also called top-lock. A double-locking tremolo also locks the strings at the bridge.

Locking tuning machines
Tuning machines that 'lock' the string in place.

Machine heads
See: *Tuning machines*.

MIDI
Musical Instrument Digital Interface. Allows communication between electronic musical devices: You can use a MIDI-guitar to trigger a synthesizer, for example.

Neck
Runs between the body and the head.

Neck pickup
The pickup closest to the neck.

Nut
Small strip between the head and the fingerboard. Important for string spacing, string height, tone, and tuning stability.

Open tuning
Another way of tuning your guitar.

Parallel
Pickups can be wired in parallel or in series.

Passive instruments
Instruments without active electronics. See: *Active EQ* and *Active pickup*s.

Phase
Humbuckers (or two single coils) can be wired in or out of phase.

Pickguard
Protects the body from being scratched by the pick or plectrum.

Pickup
Picks up the strings' vibrations and converts them into electrical signals.

Pickup selector
Allows you to select the pickup(s) you want to use for a specific type of sound.

Piezo pickup
Pressure-sensitive pickup, typically used for electric-acoustic guitars, but also (as an extra, usually) on some electric (bass) guitars.

Plain strings
The two or three unwound strings on a guitar. See also: *Wound strings*.

Position markers
Position markers mark the 3rd, 5th, 7th, 9th, and 12th (etc.) positions or frets on your instrument.

Pot, potentiometer
The electrical controls found under the volume and tone controls.
A trim pot is a small pot that is normally mounted inside the instrument's control cavity.

Radius
Indicates the exact curvature of the fingerboard.

Reverse headstock
A reverse headstock makes the treble strings shorter, and the bass strings longer, affecting both sound and playability.

Round-wound strings
String wound with a thin, rounded wire. Most guitars have round-wound bass strings, and bassists typically uses roundwounds too. See also: *Flat-wound strings*.

Saddles
Most bridges have individually adjustable saddles to set intonation, string height, and (sometimes) string spacing.

Scale
Double the distance from the nut to the 12th fret. Important for the sound and the playability of the instrument.

Semi-hollow, semi-solid
Confusing terms, commonly used to refer to a wide variety of guitar models that have one or more (humbucking) pickups, a large or a shallow soundbox, or one or two small resonance chambers.

Series
See: *Parallel.*

Single-coil pickup
Produces a brighter, cleaner, tighter sound than a dual-coil pickup or humbucker. See also: *Humbucker.*

Soundbox
The hollow 'box' or chamber that acoustically amplifies the sound of an acoustic instrument.

Staggered pickups
Pickups with pole pieces at varying heights.

Staggered tuning machines
Tuning machines with posts of varying lengths.

Stop tailpiece, stopbar tailpiece
A separate tailpiece, mounted on the instrument's top.

String height
The distance between the strings and the 12th fret. Often referred to as action. See: *Action.*

String pull
Effect caused by too-strong pickup magnets or badly adjusted pickups, disturbing the strings' vibrations.

String tree
Holds down the thinner strings so they don't buzz at, or pop out of, the nut.

String winder
Speeds up (un)winding strings.

Tailpiece
On some instruments, the strings are attached to a tailpiece, instead of to the bridge.

Thinline
Hollow-body with a shallow soundbox. Also called slimline.

Through-neck
A full-length neck that extends down the body to the tail.

Tilted headstock
A (backward) tilted headstock eliminates the need for string trees.

Toggle switch
Usually a three-way pickup selector (1. neck pickup; 2. both pickups; 3. bridge pickup). Also known as leaf switch.

Tremolo system
A bridge or tailpiece with an arm (the tremolo bar or whammy bar) that allows you to alter the tension of your strings by bending the pitch up or down. Also called vibrato (which is one of the effects you actually produce with a 'tremolo'), or whammy.
A tremolo guitar is a guitar with a trem; a hard-tail guitar has no tremolo system.

Trim pot
See: *Pot, potentiometer.*

Truss rod
Adjustable rod(s) in the neck. The truss rod counteracts the strings' tension.

Tuner
1. Electronic device that helps you tune. 2. See: *Tuning machine.*

Tuning machines
Open, closed, or sealed machines to tune your strings with. Also called tuners, (tuning) gears, (tuning) pegs, or machine heads.

Vibrato, vibrato unit
See: *Tremolo.*

Waist
See: *Bout.*

Whammy, whammy bar
Alternative name for the guitar's tremolo. See: *Tremolo.*

Wound strings
The thickest three or four guitar strings and all bass strings are wound with metal wire or ribbon. The added mass allows them to sound at the required low pitches. The exact type of winding affects the sound of the strings.

Zero fret
Extra fret, close to the nut.

Want to Know More?

Tipbooks supply you with basic information on the
instrument of your choice, and everything that comes
with it. Of course, there's a lot more to be found on all
subjects you came across on these pages. This section
offers a selection of magazines, books, helpful websites,
and organizations.

MAGAZINES

The magazines listed below concentrate on electric guitars, basses, or both; some include acoustic models as well. Please note that this list is not intended to be complete.

Guitar magazines

- *20th Century Guitar Magazine*, www.tcguitar.com

- *Guitar Digest*, www.guitardigest.com

- *Guitar One*, www.guitarworld.com/guitarone

- *Guitar Player*, www.guitarplayer.com

- *Guitar World*, www.guitarworld.com

- *Just Jazz Guita*r, www.justjazzguitar.com

- *Vintage Guitar Magazine*, www.vguitar.com

Bass guitar magazines

- *Bass Player*, www.bassplayer.com

- *Bassics*, www.bassics.com

- *Bass Guitar Magazine*, www.bassguitarmagazine.com

International (bass) guitar magazines

- *Australian Guitar Magazine*, www.next.com.au

- *Guitarist*, UK, www.guitarist.co.uk

- *Total Guita*r, UK, www.totalguitar.co.uk

- *Guitar Techniques*, UK, www.futurenet.co.uk

- *Guitar & Bass*, UK, www.ipcmedia.com/brands/guitar

GUITAR BOOKS

There are dozens of books on guitars and basses, including publications that focus on a specific brand, a specific era, or any other subject. The following is a very limited selection.
Dedicated bass books are listed separately. Method books are not included.

- *Complete Guitarist*, Richard Chapman (Dorling Kindersley, 1994; 191 pages; ISBN 978-1564587-114).

- *The Guitar Handbook*, Ralph Denyer (Knopf, 1992; 256 pages; ISBN 978-0679742-753).

- *The Ultimate Guitar Book*, Tony Bacon (Knopf, 1997; 192 pages; ISBN 978-0375700-903).

- *Totally Guitar: The Definitive Guide*, Tony Bacon (Thunder Bay Press, 2004; 6-8 pages, ISBN 978-1592231-997).

- *Complete Guide to Guitar and Amp Maintenance – A Practical Manual for Every Guitar Player*, Ritchie Flieger (Hal Leonard, 1994; 80 pages; ISBN 978-0793534-906).

- *Guitar Player Repair Guide*, Dan Erlewine (GPI Publications, 1990; 309 pages, ISBN 978-0879302-917).

- *Gruhn's Guide to Vintage Guitars – An Identification Guide for American Fretted Instruments*, George Gruhn, Walter Carter (Backbeat Books, 1999; 581 pages; ISBN 978-08793042-25).

- *American Guitars – An Illustrated History*, Tom Wheeler (Harper Collins, 1992; 384 pages; ISBN 978-0062731-548).

- *The Electric Guitar Sourcebook: How To Find The Sounds You Like*, Dave Hunter (Backbeat Books, 2006; 192 pages; ISBN 978-0879308-865).

- *How To Make Your Electric Guitar Play Great!*, Dan Erlewine (Backbeat Books, 2001; 133 pages; ISBN 978-0879306-014).

- *Electric Guitars: The Illustrated Encyclopedia*, Tony Bacon (Thunder Bay Press, 2000; 318 pages; ISBN 978-1571452-818).

- *Blue Book of Electric Guitars*, S. P. Fjestad (Blue Book Publications, 2005, ninth edition; 1008 pages; ISBN 978-18867680-574).

- *The Guitar Player Repair Guide*, Dan Erlewine (Backbeat Books, 2007. DVD included; 322 pages; ISBN 978-0879309213).

- *2008 Official Vintage Guitar Magazine Price Guide*, Alan Greenwood and Gil Hembree (Vintage Guitar Books, 2007; 520 pages; ISBN 978-1884883194).

191

BASS BOOKS

- *The Bass Book*, Tony Bacon, Barry Moorhouse (Backbeat Books, 2008; 176 pages, ISBN 978-0879309-244).

- *101 Bass Tips: Stuff All The Pros Know And Use*, Gary Willis (Hal Leonard Corporation, 2002; 80 pages; ISBN 978-0634017-476).

- *The Bass Player Book*, Karl Coryat (Backbeat Books, 1009; 224 pages; ISBN 978-0879305-734).

- *American Basses: An Illustrated History And Player's Guide To The Bass Guitar*, Jim Roberts (Backbeat Books, 2003; 210 pages, ISBN 978-0879307-219).

INTERNET

There's a lot of information available online. The following sites are some good starting points. Also check out the websites of the magazines listed above.

- www.electric-guitars.net
- www.gbase.com
- www.guitar.about.com
- www.guitar.com
- www.guitardigest.com
- www.guitarnotes.com
- www.guitarnuts.com
- www.guitarsite.com
- www.guitarstuff.co.uk
- www.jazzguitar.com
- www.newmillguitar.com
- www.wholenote.com

Bass sites

- www.12stringbass.com
- www.activebass.com

- www.altguitarbass.com
- www.basslinks.nl (bassplaza.com)
- www.talkbass.com

LOOKING FOR A TEACHER?

If you want to find a teacher online, try to search for "guitar teacher" or "bass (guitar) teacher") and the name of area or city where you live, or visit one of the following special interest websites:

- PrivateLessons.com: www.privatelessons.com
- MusicStaff.com: www.musicstaff.com
- The Music Teachers List: www.teachlist.com
- Private Music Instructor National Directory: www.oberwerk.com/pmind/pmind.htm

Tipcode List

The Tipcodes in this book offer easy access to short movies, photo series, soundtracks, and other additional information at www. tipbook.com. For your convenience, the Tipcodes in this Tipbook have been listed below.

Tipcode	Topic	Page	Chapter
EGTR-001	String pitches guitar: E, A, D, G, B, E	10	2
EGTR-002	String pitches bass: E, A, D, G	10	2
EGTR-003	Tremolo: vibrato and pitch bend	12, 67	2, 5
EGTR-004	Clean and distorted	18	2
EGTR-005	Effects	21	2
EGTR-006	Fretted & fretless bass guitar	60	5
EGTR-007	Bridge and neck pickups	73	5
EGTR-008	Humbucker and single-coil pickup	74	5
EGTR-009	Fitting new strings	113	7
EGTR-010	Stabilizing strings	115	7
EGTR-011	String pitches guitar (reference pitches)	128	9
EGTR-012	String pitches bass (reference pitches)	128	9
EGTR-013	A=440	132	9
EGTR-014	Tuning: string to string	133	9
EGTR-015	Tuning fork	135	9
EGTR-016	Tuning with harmonics	136	9
EGTR-017	Beats	137	9
EGTR-018	Adjusting intonation	151	10
EGTR-019	Moving saddle; pitch changes	152	10
EGTR-020	Double bass	166	12
EGTR-021	Classical and steel-string guitars	167	12

Tipbook Chord
Diagrams

*This chapter features chord diagrams of a large variety
of popular guitar chords. Each chord is of course
shown in both beginner and advanced positions. An
introduction on how chords are constructed is also
included!*

As explained in Chapter 3, a chord diagram shows you where to fret the strings to play a specific chord. Basic chord diagrams allow you to easily learn to play hundreds, if not thousands of popular songs.

Diagrams

The chord diagrams on pages 190–220 show you a lot more than where to put your fingers.

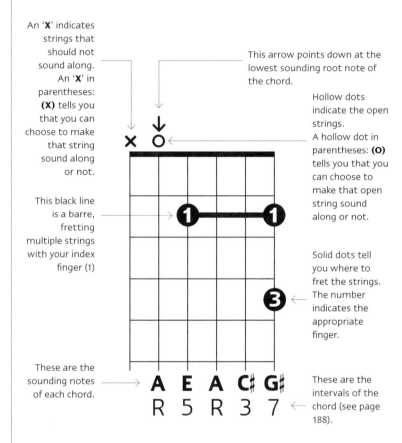

An '**X**' indicates strings that should not sound along. An '**X**' in parentheses: **(X)** tells you that you can choose to make that string sound along or not.

This black line is a barre, fretting multiple strings with your index finger (1)

These are the sounding notes of each chord.

This arrow points down at the lowest sounding root note of the chord.

Hollow dots indicate the open strings. A hollow dot in parentheses: **(O)** tells you that you can choose to make that open string sound along or not.

Solid dots tell you where to fret the strings. The number indicates the appropriate finger.

These are the intervals of the chord (see page 188).

A E A C♯ G♯
R 5 R 3 7

Tabs

Chords can be written down using tabs too, the figures indicating where to fret the strings. The first figure or symbol refers to the low E-string, the second to the A-string, and so on. A '0' indicates an open string; an 'X' indicates strings that should

not be played. This way, the upper D7 chord on page 200 looks as
follows: X-X-0-2-1-2.

Vertical tabs

Some prefer a vertical tab notation, either from low E to high E
or the other way around. Here's a brief chord progression.

		Chords		
		A7	**D7**	**E7**
Strings	E	0	2	0
	B	2	1	0
	G	0	2	1
	D	2	0	0
	A	0	X	2
	E	(0)	X	0

Chord construction

There are many different types of chords: major chords, minor
chords, diminished chords, and so on. Every specific type of
chord is constructed the same way, using a root note and two or
more other notes. How this works is explained on pages 188–189.

Table

The table on pages 186–187 shows the names, the chord
symbols, and the intervals of a variety of chord types, including
an example (in C) for each type of chord. The chords in the
lower section of this table have not been included in the chord
diagrams in this book.

Inversions

Each chord can be played in various ways. These so-called
inversions can make a chord sound higher or lower — depending
on how high it is on the neck — but they also make chords sound
differently, with another timbre or nature. You can use this
musically, of course, by choosing your chords and inversions so
that your chord progressions get a nice flow, for example. Other
than that, knowing the various ways to play each chord can make

197

Chord symbol		
C	–	C, E, G
Cmaj^7		
C7	Cdom^7	C, E, G, B♭
C6		
C9	–	C, E, G, B♭, D
Cm		
Cm^7	C–^{7}, Cmi^7, Cmin^7	C, E♭, G, B♭
Cm^9		
Csus4	Csus	C, F, G
Cadd9		
C7sus4	–	C, F, G, B♭
Csus2		
Caug	C+, C^{+5}, C$^{♯5}$	C, E, G♯
Cdim		
C$^{♭5}$	–	C, E, G♭
C7$^{♭9}$		
Cm^6	C–^{6}, Cmin^6	C, E♭, G, A
Cm$^{7(♭5)}$		
Cmi^{ma7}	C–$^\Delta$, Cm$^\Delta$, Cm$^{(maj7)}$	C, E♭, G, B

it easier to go from one chord to the next. The chord diagrams presented in this book show both the basic chord and various inversions for each chord.

TIP

> ### Beginner's chords
> In some cases, inversions are easier to play than the basic chords shown in the upper rows on pages 190–213. Still, beginners are adviced to initially focus on those 'upper' chords.

Powerchords

Page 214 shows various *powerchords*. These are relatively easy to play, 'powerful' chords consisting of the root note and the fifth of a chord only. You can play them on no more than two strings,

198

1, 3, 5	C major
1, 3, 5, ♭7	C seven, C dominant seven
1, 3, 5, ♭7, 9	C nine
1, ♭3, 5, ♭7	C minor seven
1, 4, 5	C suspended (four)
1, 4, 5, ♭7	C seven sus four
1, 3, ♯5	C augmented
1, 3, ♭5	C flat five
1, ♭3, 5, 6	C minor six
1, ♭3, 5, 7	C minor/major seven

but most players use three, sounding one or two root notes (an octave apart) and one or two fifths (also an octave apart).

More chords

- Pages 215–219 show a number of movable chords, both with and without barre.

- Numerous songs use no more than three different chords. How this works and which chords such songs often use is explained on page 221.

- Some examples of popular chord progressions in various styles of music can be found on pages 222–225.

- You can find many more chords (and tabs, etc.) online. Some interesting websites are listed on page 225.

CHORD CONSTRUCTION

Chord construction is not really that complex. Each chord has a root note.

- In C major, C minor, C dim or any other C chord, the root note is C.

- In C major, the second note of the chord sounds a major third higher than the root note (E).

- In C major, the third note of the chord sounds a perfect fifth higher than the root note (G).

If you put these steps in a row, C major looks like R (root) – 3 (major third) – 5 (perfect fifth).

Minor chords
In a minor chord, the second step is a minor third rather than a major third. This means that the second note of the chord is lowered by a half step. C minor is C–E♭–G (R–♭3–5).

Diminished, augmented
In a diminished chord, the fifth is also lowered (R–♭3–♭5); an augmented chord has a raised fifth (R–3–♯5). So each type of chord has its own specific construction.

Four
All chords listed so far are made up of three notes. There are also chords that use four or more notes, the extra notes being added to the three notes of the basic chord. These extra notes are often indicated using digits. The table on pages 186–187 includes some examples of these types of chords.

- The digit 7 in a chord symbol tells you to add a minor seventh to the chord. C7 is C–E–G–B♭ (R–3–5–♭7).

- The addition maj7 adds a major seventh to the chord (C–E–G–B or R–3–5–7).

200

- A 6 tells you to add a major sixth (C–E–G–A or R–3–5–6).

- Other additions speak for themselves. A♭5 lowers the fifth a half step (C–E–G♭); a 9 adds a high D (and a B♭) to the C-chord, ♭9 adds a D♭ and ♯9 a D♯, and so on. There are also 11 and 13 chords.

- Some chord inversions can make it necessary or desirable to leave out certain notes of a chord, such as the 5, the 7 or even the root note. If there's no root note in a chord, this can be indicated by the letters NR (no root).

A

| A | Amaj7 | A7 | A6 | A9 |

Barre ❶–❶
Fret with 2nd finger ❷
Fretting is optional ❹
Fret with thumb ⓣ
Lowest root note ↓
Don't play this string ×
Open string o
Don't play (optional) (x)
Open string (optional) (O)

A

E A E A C♯ E
5 R 5 R 3 5

E A E A C♯ A
5 R 5 R 3 R

A E A C♯ E A
R 5 R 3 5 R

A A C♯ E A
R R 3 5 R

A C♯ E A E
R 3 5 R 5

Amaj7

E A E G♯ C♯ E
5 R 5 7 3 5

E A E A C♯ G♯
5 R 5 R 3 7

A G♯ C♯ E
R 7 3 5

A A C♯ E G♯
R R 3 5 7

A C♯ E G♯ C♯
R 3 5 7 3

A7

E A E G C♯ E
5 R 5 ♭7 3 5

E A E A C♯ G
5 R 5 R 3 ♭7

A E G C♯ E A
R 5 ♭7 3 5 R

A A C♯ G A
R R 3 ♭7 R

A C♯ G A E
R 3 ♭7 R 5

A6

E A F♯ A C♯ E
5 R 6 R 3 5

E A E A C♯ F♯
5 R 5 R 3 6

A E G C♯ F♯ A
R 5 ♭7 3 6 R

A A C♯ F♯ A
R R 3 6 R

A C♯ F♯ A
R 3 6 R

A9

E A G B C♯ E
5 R ♭7 9 3 5

E A E B C♯ G
5 R 5 9 3 ♭7

A E G C♯ E B
R 5 ♭7 3 5 9

A A C♯ G B
R R 3 ♭7 9

A C♯ G B E
R 3 ♭7 9 5

5 | 5 | 5 | 5 | 5
5 | 4 | 5 | 5 | 6
9 | 9 | 10 | 10 | 11

202

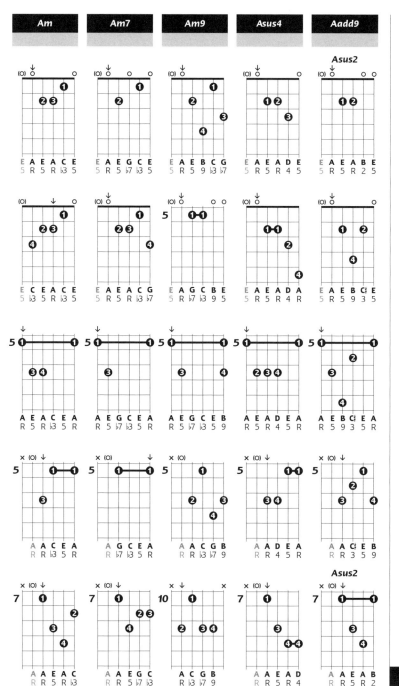

A

Am | Am7 | Am9 | Asus4 | Aadd9

B♭

Enharmonic: **A♯**

Barre	
Fret with 2nd finger	❷
Fretting is optional	❹
Fret with thumb	Ⓣ
Lowest root note	↓
Don't play this string	✕
Open string	o
Don't play (optional)	(✕)
Open string (optional)	(O)

B♭   **B♭maj7**   **B♭7**   **B♭6**   **B♭9**

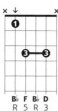
B♭ F B♭ D
R 5 R 3

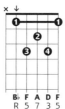
B♭ F A D F
R 5 7 3 5

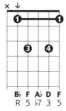
B♭ F A♭ D F
R 5 ♭7 3 5

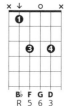
B♭ F G D
R 5 6 3

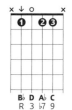
B♭ D A♭ C
R 3 ♭7 9

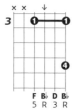
F B♭ D B♭
5 R 3 R

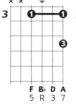
F B♭ D A
5 R 3 7

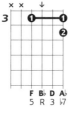
F B♭ D A♭
5 R 3 ♭7

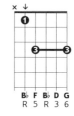
B♭ F B♭ D G
R 5 R 3 6

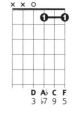
D A♭ C F
3 ♭7 9 5

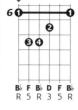
B♭ F B♭ D F B♭
R 5 R 3 5 R

B♭ A D F
R 7 3 5

B♭ F A♭ D F B♭
R 5 ♭7 3 5 R

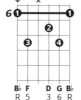
B♭ F D G B♭
R 5 3 6 R

B♭ F A♭ D F C
R 5 ♭7 3 5 9

B♭ D F B♭
R 3 5 R

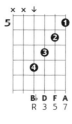
B♭ D F A
R 3 5 7

B♭ D A♭ B♭
R 3 ♭7 R

B♭ D G B♭
R 3 6 R

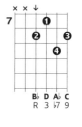
B♭ D A♭ C
R 3 ♭7 9

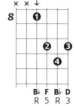
B♭ F B♭ D
R 5 R 3

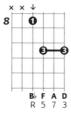
B♭ F A D
R 5 7 3

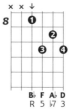
B♭ F A♭ D
R 5 ♭7 3

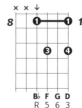
B♭ F G D
R 5 6 3

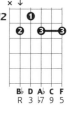
B♭ D A♭ C F
R 3 ♭7 9 5

B♭

Enharmonic: **A♯**

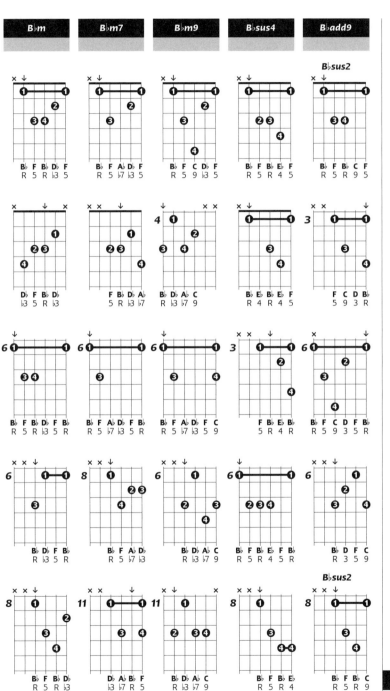

B♭m	B♭m7	B♭m9	B♭sus4	B♭add9

B

| B | Bmaj7 | B7 | B6 | B9 |

Legend:

Barre	❶–❶
Fret with 2nd finger	❷
Fretting is optional	④
Fret with thumb	Ⓣ
Lowest root note	↓
Don't play this string	×
Open string	o
Don't play (optional)	(×)
Open string (optional)	(O)

Row 1:

B
B F♯ B D♯
R 5 R 3

Bmaj7
B F♯ A♯ D♯ F♯
R 5 7 3 5

B7
B D♯ A B F♯
R 3 ♭7 R 5

B6
B D♯ G♯ B F♯
R 3 6 R 5

B9
B D♯ A C♯
R 3 ♭7 9

Row 2:

4 — F♯ B D♯ B
5 R 3 R

4 — F♯ B D♯ A♯
5 R 3 7

B7 — B F♯ A D♯ F♯
R 5 ♭7 3 5

B6 — B F♯ B D♯ G♯
R 5 R 3 6

B9 — B D♯ A C♯ F♯
R 3 ♭7 9 5

Row 3:

7 — B F♯ B D♯ F♯ B
R 5 R 3 5 R

7 — B A♯ D♯ F♯
R 7 3 5

7 — B A D♯ F♯
R ♭7 3 5

6 — B G♯ D♯ F♯
R 6 3 5

6 — D♯ A C♯ F♯ B
3 ♭7 9 5 R

Row 4:

7 — B D♯ F♯ B
R 3 5 R

6 — B D♯ F♯ A♯
R 3 5 7

7 — B D♯ A B
R 3 ♭7 R

7 — B D♯ G♯ B
R 3 6 R

7 — B F♯ A D♯ F♯ B
R 5 ♭7 3 5 9

Row 5:

9 — B F♯ B D♯
R 5 R 3

9 — B F♯ A♯ D♯
R 5 7 3

9 — B F♯ A D♯
R 5 ♭7 3

9 — B F♯ G♯ D♯
R 5 6 3

8 — B D♯ A C♯
R 3 ♭7 9

206

B

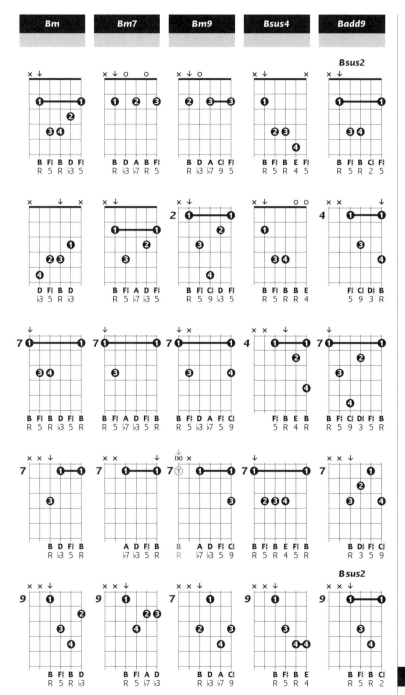

Bm	Bm7	Bm9	Bsus4	Badd9

C

C	Cmaj7	C7	C6	C9

Legend:

Barre	❶-❶
Fret with 2nd finger	❷
Fretting is optional	④
Fret with thumb	Ⓣ
Lowest root note	↓
Don't play this string	×
Open string	o
Don't play (optional)	(×)
Open string (optional)	(O)

Row 1:

C: E C E G C E / 3 R 3 5 R 3

Cmaj7: E C E G B E / 3 R 3 5 7 3

C7: E C E B♭ C E / 3 R 3 ♭7 R 3

C6: E C E A C E / 3 R 3 6 R 3

C9: E C E B♭ D E / 3 R 3 ♭7 9 3

Row 2:

C: C G C E G / R 5 R 3 5

Cmaj7: C G B E G / R 5 7 3 5

C7: C G B♭ E G / R 5 ♭7 3 5

C6: C G A E E / R 5 6 3 3

C9: E C E B♭ D G / 3 R 3 ♭7 9 5

Row 3:

C (5): G C E C / 5 R 3 R

Cmaj7 (5): G C E B / 5 R 3 7

C7 (5): G C E B♭ / 5 R 3 ♭7

C6: C G C E A / R 5 R 3 6

C9 (7): E B♭ D G C / 3 ♭7 9 5 R

Row 4:

C (8): C G C E G C / R 5 R 3 5 R

Cmaj7 (8): C B E G / R 7 3 5

C7 (8): C G B♭ E B♭ C / R 5 ♭7 3 ♭7 R

C6 (8): C G E A C / R 5 3 6 R

C9 (8): C G B♭ E G D / R 5 ♭7 3 5 9

Row 5:

C (8): C E G C / R 3 5 R

Cmaj7 (7): C E G B / R 3 5 7

C7 (8): C E B♭ C / R 3 ♭7 R

C6 (8): C E A C / R 3 6 R

C9 (9): C E B♭ D / R 3 ♭7 9

208

Cm	Cm7	Cm9	Csus4	Cadd9

C

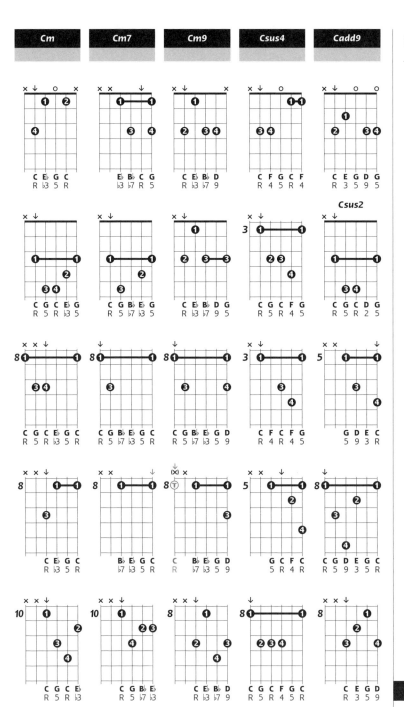

D♭

Enharmonic: **C♯**

Barre	
Fret with 2nd finger	❷
Fretting is optional	④
Fret with thumb	Ⓣ
Lowest root note	↓
Don't play this string	×
Open string	o
Don't play (optional)	(×)
Open string (optional)	(O)

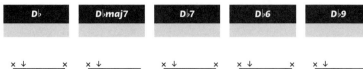

D♭	D♭maj7	D♭7	D♭6	D♭9

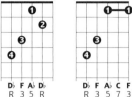 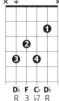 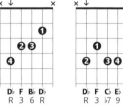

Row 1

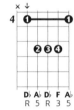
D♭ F A♭ D♭
R 3 5 R

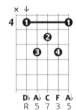
D♭ F A♭ C F
R 3 5 7 3

D♭ F C♭ D♭
R 3 ♭7 R

D♭ F B♭ D♭
R 3 6 R

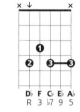
D♭ F C♭ E♭
R 3 ♭7 9

Row 2

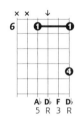
D♭ A♭ D♭ F A♭
R 5 R 3 5

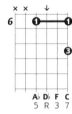
D♭ A♭ C F A♭
R 5 7 3 5

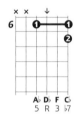
D♭ A♭ C♭ F A♭
R 5 ♭7 3 5

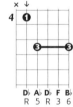
D♭ A♭ B♭ F
R 5 6 3

D♭ F C♭ E♭ A♭
R 3 ♭7 9 5

Row 3

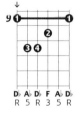
A♭ D♭ F D♭
5 R 3 R

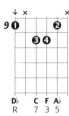
A♭ D♭ F C
5 R 3 7

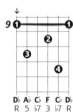
A♭ D♭ F C♭
5 R 3 ♭7

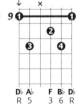
D♭ A♭ D♭ F B♭
R 5 R 3 6

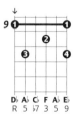
F C♭ E♭ A♭ D♭
3 ♭7 9 5 R

Row 4

D♭ A♭ D♭ F A♭ D♭
R 5 R 3 5 R

D♭   C F A♭
R   7 3 5

D♭ A♭ C♭ F C♭ D♭
R 5 ♭7 3 ♭7 R

D♭ A♭   F B♭ D♭
R 5   3 6 R

D♭ A♭ C♭ F A♭ E♭
R 5 ♭7 3 5 9

Row 5

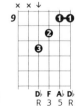
D♭ F A♭ D♭
R 3 5 R

D♭ F A♭ C
R 3 5 7

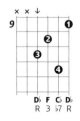
D♭ F C♭ D♭
R 3 ♭7 R

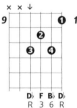
D♭ F B♭ D♭
R 3 6 R

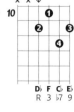
D♭ F C♭ E♭
R 3 ♭7 9

D♭

Enharmonic: **C♯**

D♭m	D♭m7	D♭m9	D♭sus4	D♭add9

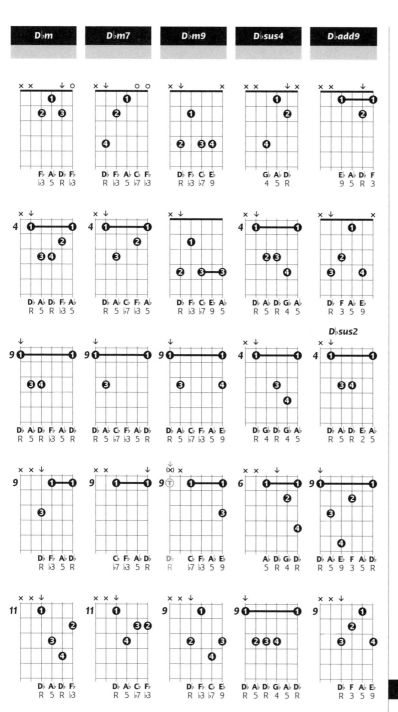

D♭sus2

D

D	Dmaj7	D7	D6	D9

Legend

Barre	❶–❶
Fret with 2nd finger	❷
Fretting is optional	❹
Fret with thumb	Ⓣ
Lowest root note	↓
Don't play this string	×
Open string	o
Don't play (optional)	(×)
Open string (optional)	(O)

Row 1

D: A D A D F♯ / 5 R 5 R 3
Dmaj7: A D A C♯ F♯ / 5 R 5 7 3
D7: A D A C F♯ / 5 R 5 ♭7 3
D6: A D A B F♯ / 5 R 5 6 3
D9: A F♯ A C E / 5 3 5 ♭7 9

Row 2

D: D F♯ A D F♯ / R 3 5 R 3
Dmaj7: D F♯ A C♯ F♯ / R 3 5 7 3
D7: D F♯ C D / R 3 ♭7 R
D6: D F♯ B D / R 3 6 R
D9: D C E A / R ♭7 9 5

Row 3

D (5): D A D F♯ / R 5 R 3
Dmaj7 (5): D A C♯ F♯ A / R 5 7 3 5
D7 (5): D A C F♯ A / R 5 ♭7 3 5
D6 (4): D F♯ B F♯ / R 3 6 3
D9 (4): D F♯ C E / R 3 ♭7 9

Row 4

D (5): D D F♯ A / R R 3 5
Dmaj7 (7): A D F♯ C♯ / 5 R 3 7
D7 (7): A D F♯ C / 5 R 3 ♭7
D6 (5): D A D F♯ B / R 5 R 3 6
D9 (4): D F♯ C E A / R 3 ♭7 9 5

Row 5

D (10): D A D F♯ A D / R 5 R 3 5 R
Dmaj7 (10): D C♯ F♯ A / R 7 3 5
D7 (10): D C F♯ A / R ♭7 3 5
D6 (9): D B F♯ A / R 6 3 5
D9 (10): D A C F♯ A E / R 5 ♭7 3 5 9

212

D

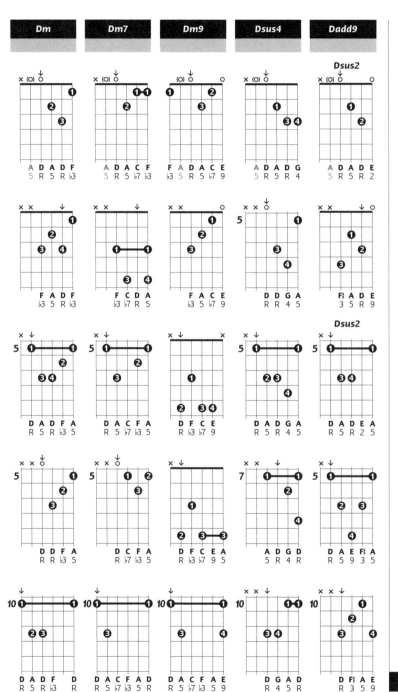

Dm	Dm7	Dm9	Dsus4	Dadd9

Dsus2

A D A D F
5 R 5 R ♭3

A D A C F
5 R 5 ♭7 ♭3

F A D A C E
♭3 5 R 5 ♭7 9

A D A D G
5 R 5 R 4

A D A D E
5 R 5 R 2

F A D F
♭3 5 R ♭3

F C D A
♭3 ♭7 R 5

F A C E
♭3 5 ♭7 9

D D G A
R R 4 5

F♯ A D E
3 5 R 9

Dsus2

D A D F A
R 5 R ♭3 5

D A C F A
R 5 ♭7 ♭3 5

D F C E
R ♭3 ♭7 9

D A D G A
R 5 R 4 5

D A D E A
R 5 R 2 5

D D F A
R R ♭3 5

D C F A
R ♭7 ♭3 5

D F C E A
R ♭3 ♭7 9 5

A D G D
5 R 4 R

D A E F♯ A
R 5 9 3 5

D A D F   D
R 5 R ♭3   R

D A C F A D
R 5 ♭7 ♭3 5 R

D A C F A E
R 5 ♭7 ♭3 5 9

D G A D
R 4 5 R

D F♯ A E
R 3 5 9

213

E♭

Enharmonic: **D♯**

Barre	
Fret with 2nd finger	❷
Fretting is optional	④
Fret with thumb	Ⓣ
Lowest root note	↓
Don't play this string	×
Don't play (optional)	(×)
Open string	o
Open string (optional)	(O)

E♭	E♭maj7	E♭7	E♭6	E♭9
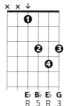 E♭ B♭ E♭ G R 5 R 3	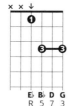 E♭ B♭ D G R 5 7 3	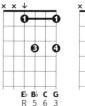 E♭ B♭ D♭ G R 5 ♭7 3	 E♭ B♭ C G R 5 6 3	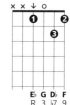 E♭ G D♭ F R 3 ♭7 9
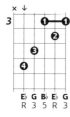 E♭ G B♭ E♭ G R 3 5 R 3	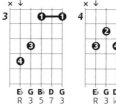 E♭ G B♭ D G R 3 5 7 3	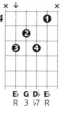 E♭ G D♭ E♭ R 3 ♭7 R	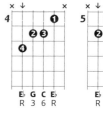 E♭ G C E♭ R 3 6 R	 E♭ G D♭ F R 3 ♭7 9
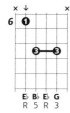 E♭ B♭ E♭ G R 5 R 3	 E♭ B♭ D G B♭ R 5 7 3 5	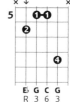 E♭ B♭ D♭ G B♭ R 5 ♭7 3 5	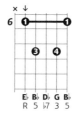 E♭ G C G R 3 6 3	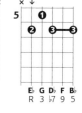 E♭ G D♭ F B♭ R 3 ♭7 9 5
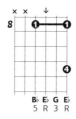 B♭ E♭ G E♭ 5 R 3 R	 B♭ E♭ G D 5 R 3 7	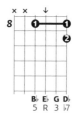 B♭ E♭ G D♭ 5 R 3 ♭7	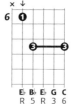 E♭ B♭ E♭ G C R 5 R 3 6	 G D♭ F B♭ E♭ 3 ♭7 9 5 R
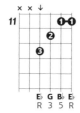 E♭ G B♭ E♭ R 3 5 R	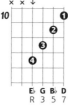 E♭ G B♭ D R 3 5 7	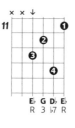 E♭ G D♭ E♭ R 3 ♭7 R	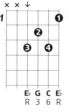 E♭ G C E♭ R 3 6 R	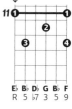 E♭ B♭ D♭ G B♭ F R 5 ♭7 3 5 9

214

| E♭m | E♭m7 | E♭m9 | E♭sus4 | E♭add9 |

E♭

Enharmonic: **D♯**

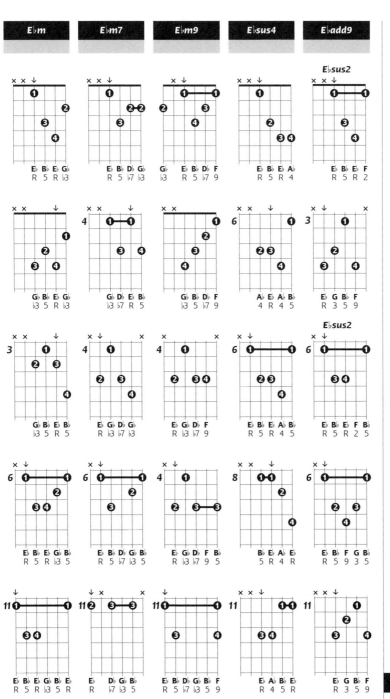

E

Barre	❶–❶
Fret with 2nd finger	❷
Fretting is optional	❹
Fret with thumb	Ⓣ
Lowest root note	↓
Don't play this string	×
Open string	o
Don't play (optional)	(×)
Open string (optional)	(O)

E	Emaj7	E7	E6	E9

Chord diagrams:

Row 1:
- E: E B E G# B E / R 5 R 3 5 R
- Emaj7: E B D# G# B E / R 5 7 3 5 R
- E7: E B D G# B E / R 5 ♭7 3 5 R
- E6: E C# E G# B E / R 6 R 3 5 R
- E9: E B D G# B F# / R 5 ♭7 3 5 9

Row 2:
- E: E B E B E G# / R 5 R 5 R 3
- Emaj7: E B E G# D# / R 5 R 3 7
- E7: E B E G# D E / R 5 R 3 ♭7 R
- E6: E B E G# C# E / R 5 R 3 6 R
- E9: E B D G# D F# / R 5 ♭7 3 ♭7 9

Row 3:
- E (4): E E G# B E G# / R R 3 5 R 3
- Emaj7 (4): E E G# B D# E / R R 3 5 7 R
- E7 (5): E E G# D E E / R R 3 ♭7 R R
- E6 (6): E E G# C# B E / R R 3 6 5 R
- E9 (6): E E G# D F# E / R R 3 ♭7 9 R

Row 4:
- E (7): B E B E G# B / 5 R 5 R 3 5
- Emaj7 (7): B E B D# G# B / 5 R 5 7 3 5
- E7 (7): E E B D G# B / R R 5 ♭7 3 5
- E6 (7): E E B E G# C# / R R 5 R 3 6
- E9 (6): E E G# D F# B / R R 3 ♭7 9 5

Row 5:
- E (9): E G# B E G# E / R 3 5 R 3 R
- Emaj7 (9): E B E G# D# / R 5 R 3 7
- E7 (9): E B E G# D / R 5 R 3 ♭7
- E6 (11): E C# G# B / R 6 3 5
- E9 (11): E G# D F# B E / R 3 ♭7 9 5 R

216

Em	Em7	Em9	Esus4	Eadd9

E

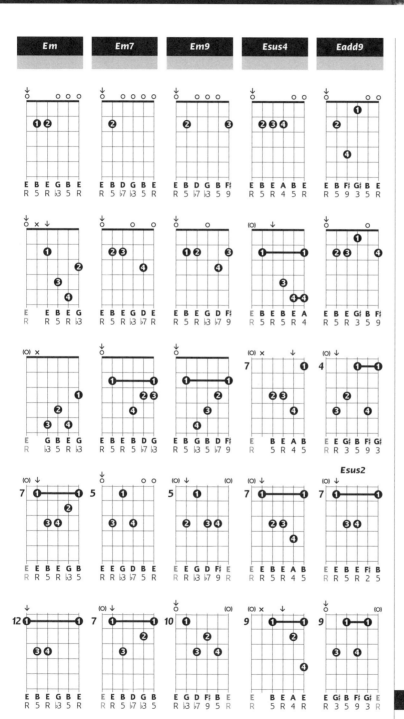

F

F	Fmaj7	F7	F6	F9

Chord diagrams for F, Fmaj7, F7, F6, F9 in multiple positions.

F	Fmaj7	F7	F6	F9
A F A C F 3 R 3 5 R	A F A C E 3 R 3 5 7	A F A E♭ F 3 R 3 ♭7 R	A F A D F 3 R 3 6 R	A F A E♭ G 3 R 3 ♭7 9
F C F A C F R 5 R 3 5 R	F A E A C E R 3 7 3 5 7	F C E♭ A C F R 5 ♭7 3 5 R	F C A D F R 5 3 6 R	F C E♭ A C G R 5 ♭7 3 5 9
F A C F R 3 5 R	F A C E A R 3 5 7 3	F A E♭ F R 3 ♭7 R	F A D F R 3 6 R	F A E♭ G R 3 ♭7 9
F C F A R 5 R 3	F C E A C R 5 7 3 5	F C E♭ A C R 5 ♭7 3 5	F C F A D R 5 R 3 6	F A E♭ G C R 3 ♭7 9 5
C F A F 5 R 3 R	C F A E 5 R 3 7	C F A E♭ 5 R 3 ♭7	F A C F A D R 3 5 R 3 6	A E♭ G C F 3 ♭7 9 5 R

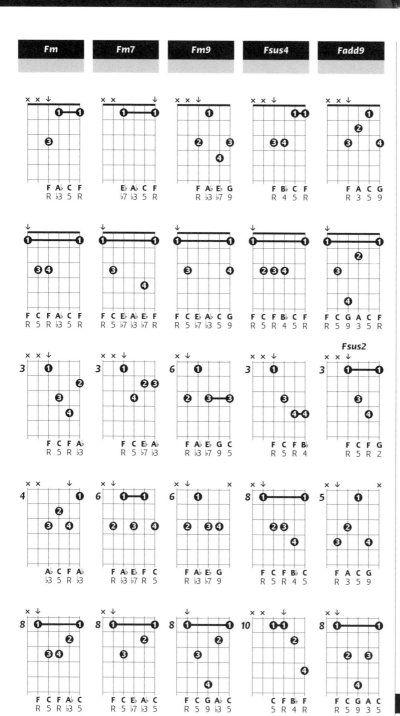

Fm · **Fm7** · **Fm9** · **Fsus4** · **Fadd9**

F

F♯

Enharmonic: **G♭**

Barre	**❶–❶**
Fret with 2nd finger	**❷**
Fretting is optional	**❹**
Fret with thumb	**Ⓣ**
Lowest root note	↓
Don't play this string	×
Open string	o
Don't play (optional)	(×)
Open string (optional)	(O)

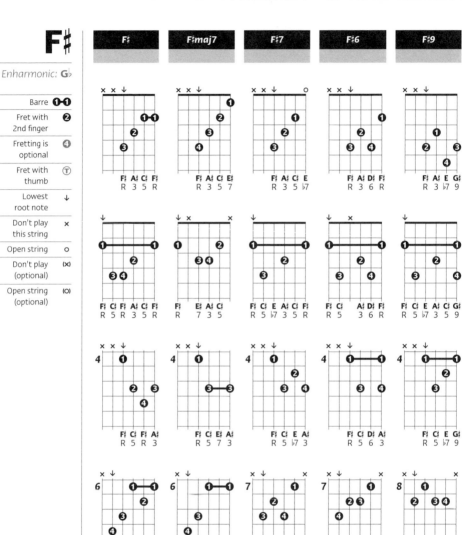

F#

Enharmonic: **G♭**

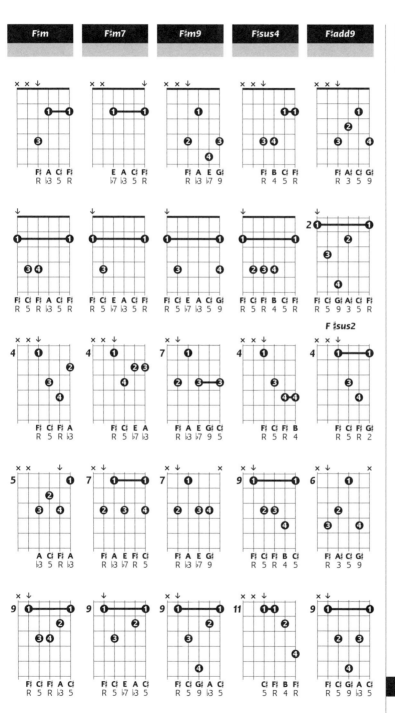

F#m	F#m7	F#m9	F#sus4	F#add9

F# A C# F#
R ♭3 5 R

E A C# F#
♭7 ♭3 5 R

F# A E G#
R ♭3 ♭7 9

F# B C# F#
R 4 5 R

F# A C# G#
R 3 5 9

F# C# F# A C# F#
R 5 R ♭3 5 R

F# C# E A C# F#
R 5 ♭7 ♭3 5 R

F# C# E A C# F#
R 5 ♭7 ♭3 5 9

F# C# E B C# F#
R 5 R 4 5 R

F# C# G# A# C# F#
R 5 9 3 5 R

F#sus2

F# C# F# A
R 5 R ♭3

F# C# E A
R 5 ♭7 ♭3

F# A E G# C#
R ♭3 ♭7 9 5

F# C# F# B
R 5 R 4

F# C# F# G#
R 5 R 2

A C# F# A
♭3 5 R ♭3

F# A E F# C#
R ♭3 ♭7 R 5

F# A E G#
R ♭3 ♭7 9

F# C# F# B C#
R 5 R 4 5

F# A# C# G#
R 3 5 9

F# C# F# A C#
R 5 R ♭3 5

F# C# E A C#
R 5 ♭7 ♭3 5

F# C# G# A C#
R 5 9 ♭3 5

C# F# B F#
5 R 4 R

F# C# G# A C#
R 5 9 ♭3 5

G

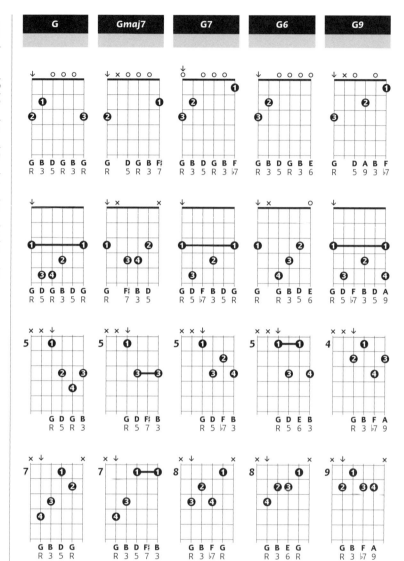

Barre	❶–❶
Fret with 2nd finger	❷
Fretting is optional	④
Fret with thumb	Ⓣ
Lowest root note	↓
Don't play this string	×
Open string	o
Don't play (optional)	(×)
Open string (optional)	(O)

G

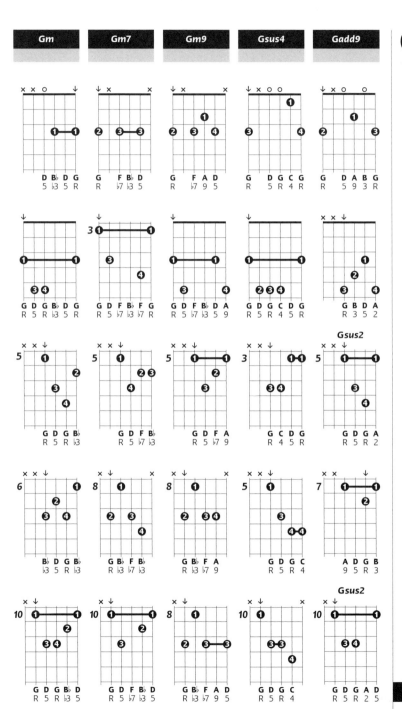

A♭

Enharmonic: **G♯**

Barre	
Fret with 2nd finger	❷
Fretting is optional	❹
Fret with thumb	Ⓣ
Lowest root note	↓
Don't play this string	×
Open string	o
Don't play (optional)	(×)
Open string (optional)	(O)

A♭

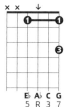

E♭ A♭ C A♭
5 R 3 R

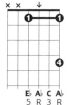

A♭ C E♭ A♭
R 3 5 R

A♭ E♭ A♭ C E♭ A♭
R 5 R 3 5 R

A♭ E♭ A♭ C
R 5 R 3

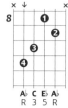

A♭ C E♭ A♭
R 3 5 R

A♭maj7

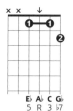

E♭ A♭ C G
5 R 3 7

A♭ C E♭ G
R 3 5 7

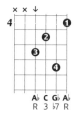

A♭ G C E♭
R 7 3 5

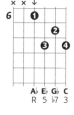

A♭ E♭ G C
R 5 7 3

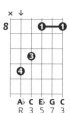

A♭ C E♭ G C
R 3 5 7 3

A♭7

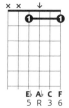

E♭ A♭ C G♭
5 R 3 ♭7

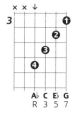

A♭ C G♭ A♭
R 3 ♭7 R

A♭ G♭ C E♭
R ♭7 3 5

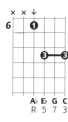

A♭ E♭ G♭ C
R 5 ♭7 3

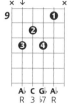

A♭ C G♭ A♭
R 3 ♭7 R

A♭6

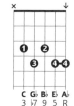

E♭ A♭ C F
5 R 3 6

A♭ C F A♭
R 3 6 R

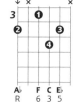

A♭ F C E♭
R 6 3 5

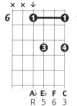

A♭ E♭ F C
R 5 6 3

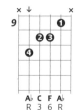

A♭ C F A♭
R 3 6 R

A♭9

C G♭ B♭ E♭ A♭
3 ♭7 9 5 R

A♭ C G♭ B♭
R 3 ♭7 9

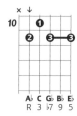

A♭ E♭ G♭ C E♭ B♭
R 5 ♭7 3 5 9

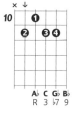

A♭ C G♭ B♭
R 3 ♭7 9

A♭ C G♭ B♭ E♭
R 3 ♭7 9 5

224

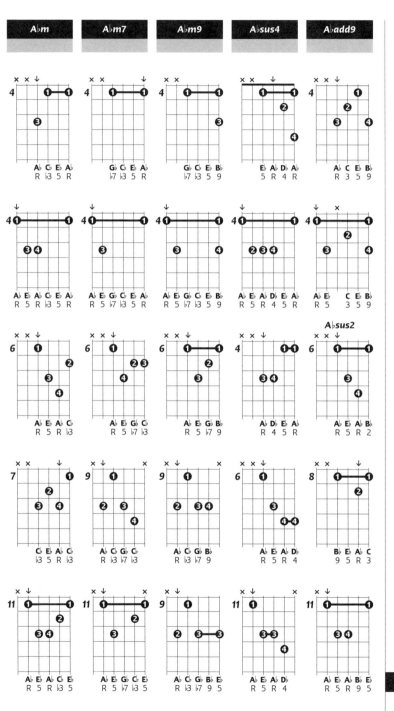

A♭

Enharmonic: **G♯**

POWERCHORDS

The powerchords (see page 186) on this page are easy to play. They're mainly used in pop and heavy metal.

OPEN POWER CHORDS

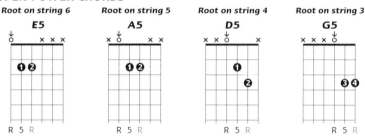

POWER CHORDS

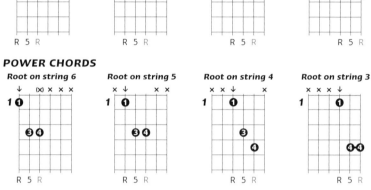

The four chords above are movable power chords in the first position (F5, A♯/B♭5, D♯/E♭5, and G♯/A♭5 respectively). Each time you move them one fret up, they will sound a half step higher. The table below shows the resulting chords in the first six positions.

1 F5	1 A♯5 – B♭5	1 D♯5–E♭5	1 G♯5 – A♭5
2 F♯5 – G♭5	2 B5	2 E5	2 A5
3 G5	3 C5	3 F5	3 A♯5 – B♭5
4 G♯5 – A♭5	4 C♯5 – D♭5	4 F♯5 – G♭5	4 B5
5 A5	5 D5	5 G5	5 C5
6 A♯5 – B♭5	6 D♯5–E♭5	6 G♯5 – A♭5	6 C♯5 – D♭5
etc.	etc.	etc.	etc.

BARRE AND MOVABLE CHORDS

There is a large group of chords that you can simply move along the neck of your instrument. Many of these *movable chords* use a barre, fretting two or more strings with your index finger. These chords are known as *movable barre chords*.

Example
The F major barre chord is a well-known example of a movable barre chord. Move the chord from the first to the second position on your guitar, and you'll hear the same chord a half step higher (F♯). Move it up another fret and you'll hear G major — and so on. The guitar necks and tables on pages 216-217 show you the root note for each position.

The top nut
F major is actually the same chord 'shape' as E major — but in E major, the top nut replaces the barre.

No barre
Other movable chord shapes do not use a barre (pages 218–219). The root note of these chords is indicated by an arrow and/or the letter R below the chord chart.

Open tuning
If a song uses one type of chords only, you can tune your guitar to that chord (open tunings; see page 125). If you do so, you can play the entire song by simply fretting all strings simultaneously (using your index finger or a slide; see page 125) and moving up and down the neck.

Examples
A large number of movable chords has already been included in the chord diagrams on the previous pages. The next four pages show you additional examples of barre and movable chords respectively.

227

Barre Chords

Basic chord

Barre chord

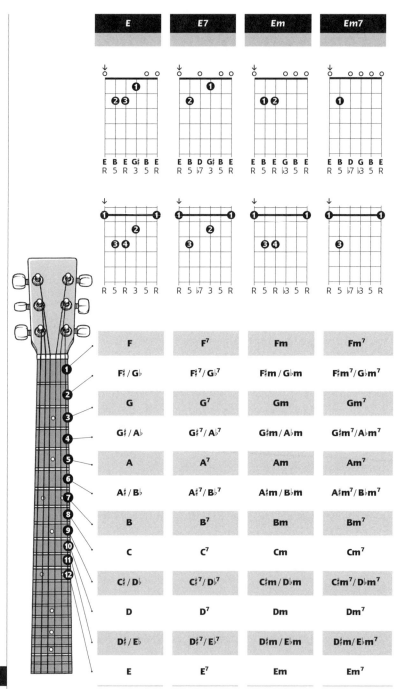

E	E7	Em	Em7

Basic chord:

E B E G♯ B E	E B D G♯ B E	E B E G B E	E B D G B E
R 5 R 3 5 R	R 5 ♭7 3 5 R	R 5 R ♭3 5 R	R 5 ♭7 ♭3 5 R

Barre chord:

R 5 R 3 5 R	R 5 ♭7 3 5 R	R 5 R ♭3 5 R	R 5 ♭7 ♭3 5 R

F	F⁷	Fm	Fm⁷
F♯/G♭	F♯⁷/G♭⁷	F♯m/G♭m	F♯m⁷/G♭m⁷
G	G⁷	Gm	Gm⁷
G♯/A♭	G♯⁷/A♭⁷	G♯m/A♭m	G♯m⁷/A♭m⁷
A	A⁷	Am	Am⁷
A♯/B♭	A♯⁷/B♭⁷	A♯m/B♭m	A♯m⁷/B♭m⁷
B	B⁷	Bm	Bm⁷
C	C⁷	Cm	Cm⁷
C♯/D♭	C♯⁷/D♭⁷	C♯m/D♭m	C♯m⁷/D♭m⁷
D	D⁷	Dm	Dm⁷
D♯/E♭	D♯⁷/E♭⁷	D♯m/E♭m	D♯m⁷/E♭m⁷
E	E⁷	Em	Em⁷

Barre Chords

A	A7	Am	Am7

Basic chord

E A E A C♯ E	E A E G C♯ E	E A E A C E	E A E G C E
5 R 5 R 3 5	5 R 5 ♭7 3 5	5 R 5 R ♭3 5	5 R 5 ♭7 ♭3 5

Barre chord

5 R 5 R 3 5	5 R 5 ♭7 3 5	5 R 5 R ♭3 5	5 R 5 ♭7 ♭3 5

A♯/B♭	A♯7/B♭7	A♯m/B♭m	A♯m7/B♭m7
B	B7	Bm	Bm7
C	C7	Cm	Cm7
C♯/D♭	C♯7/D♭7	C♯m/D♭m	C♯m7/D♭m7
D	D7	Dm	Dm7
D♯/E♭	D♯7/E♭7	D♯m/E♭m	D♯m/E♭m7
E	E7	Em	Em7
F	F7	Fm	Fm7
F♯/G♭	F♯7/G♭7	F♯m/G♭m	F♯m7/G♭m7
G	G7	Gm	Gm7
G♯/A♭	G♯7/A♭7	G♯m/A♭m	G♯m7/A♭m7
A	A7	Am	Am7

229

Movable Chords

Barre	🄍🄍
Fret with 2nd finger	❷
Fretting is optional	❹
Fret with thumb	Ⓣ
Lowest root note	↓
Don't play this string	×
Open string	o
Don't play (optional)	(×)
Open string (optional)	(O)

Major	Major	Major	9	Augmented
Root on string 6	Root on string 5	Root on string 4		

Major / **Major** / **Major**

Major 7 (Δ) / **Major 7 (Δ)** / **Major 7 (Δ)**

Dominant 7 / **Dominant 7** / **Dominant 7**

sus 4

Major 6 / **Major 6** / **Major 6**

Dom 7♯5 / **Dom 7♯5** / **Dom 7♯5**

230

Movable Chords

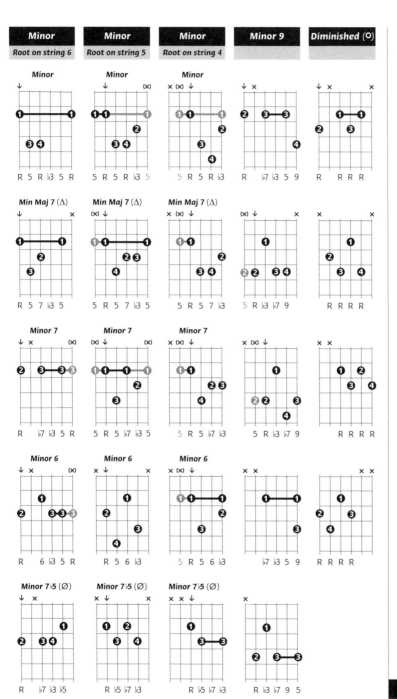

Minor	Minor	Minor	Minor 9	Diminished (O)
Root on string 6	Root on string 5	Root on string 4		

CAPO

A capo allows you to play a song any number of half steps high-er while using the same chord shapes. This can be handy if, for example, a song is too low for your vocal range, or for the singer you're playing with. Below are four examples of chords that are played with a capo at the third fret.

A capo at the second fret makes chords sound a whole step higher.

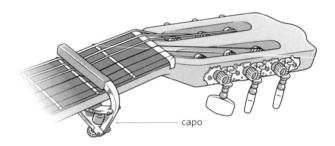

capo

Four 'open' chords, played without a capo...

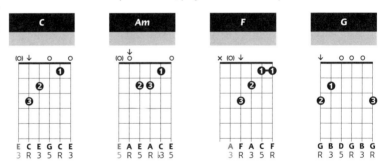

... and the same chord shapes, played *with* a capo at the third fret.

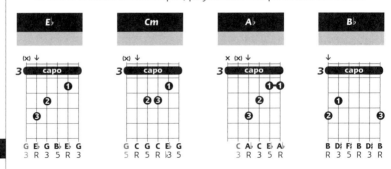

232

THREE CHORDS: I, IV, V

Many pop songs use no more than three chords. A very common chord progression uses the chords I, IV and V (one, four, five, in Roman numerals): If the first chord is C (I), the other chords in the song are F (IV) and G (V). These songs always end on the I chord, and they often start on that same chord too.

The circle of fifths, below, shows you the relationships between the chords. The IV chord is the chord left of the I chord; the V chord is the one right of the I. So if a song ends on C major, it will most probably also use F major (IV) and G major (V).

The major chords (C, G, etc.) are on the outside of the circle of fifths. The minor chords (Am, Em, etc.) are on the inside.

Minor

To add a little variation to a song, the I, IV and V chords can be replaced by the corresponding minor chords on the inside of the circle of fifths, for example, replacing C (I) by A minor, and F (IV) by D minor.

233

CHORD PROGRESSIONS

As you can imagine, I, IV, V is not the only popular chord progression. Below are some examples of common progressions in a variety of musical styles. Note that a slash (/) tells you to repeat the preceding chord. Enjoy!

Folk 1

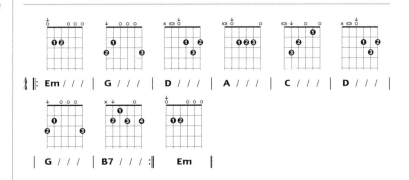

Folk 2

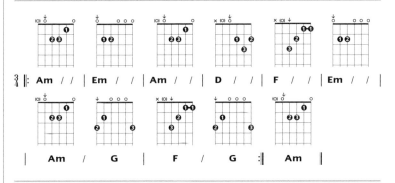

Pop 1

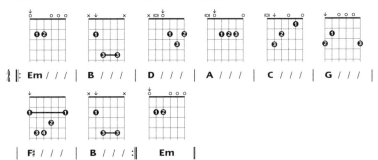

234

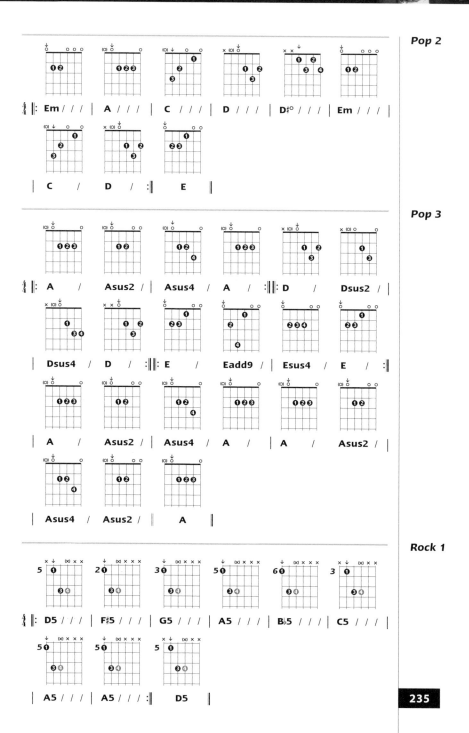

Pop 2

$\frac{4}{4}$ ‖: Em / / / | A / / / | C / / / | D / / / | D#° / / / | Em / / / |

| C / | D / :‖ E ‖

Pop 3

$\frac{4}{4}$ ‖: A / | Asus2 / | Asus4 / | A / :‖‖: D / | Dsus2 / |

| Dsus4 / | D / :‖‖: E / | Eadd9 / | Esus4 / | E / :‖

| A / | Asus2 / | Asus4 / | A / | A / | Asus2 / |

| Asus4 / | Asus2 / ‖ A ‖

Rock 1

$\frac{4}{4}$ ‖: D5 / / / | F#5 / / / | G5 / / / | A5 / / / | Bb5 / / / | C5 / / / |

| A5 / / / | A5 / / / :‖ D5 ‖

Rock 2

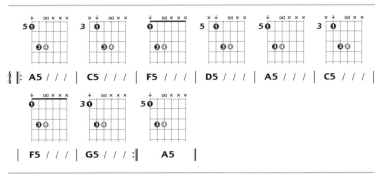

$\frac{4}{4}$ ‖: A5 / / / | C5 / / / | F5 / / / | D5 / / / | A5 / / / | C5 / / / |

| F5 / / / | G5 / / / :‖   A5   ‖

Metal 1

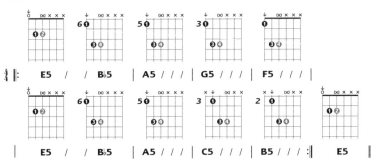

$\frac{4}{4}$ ‖:   E5 / / B♭5 | A5 / / / | G5 / / / | F5 / / / |

| E5 / / B♭5 | A5 / / / | C5 / / / | B5 / / / :‖   E5 ‖

Metal 2

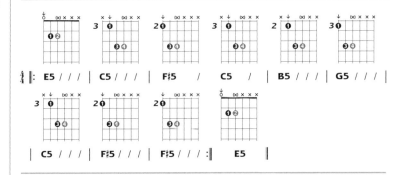

$\frac{4}{4}$ ‖: E5 / / / | C5 / / / | F♯5 /   C5 / | B5 / / / | G5 / / / |

| C5 / / / | F♯5 / / / | F♯5 / / / :‖   E5 ‖

Jazz 1

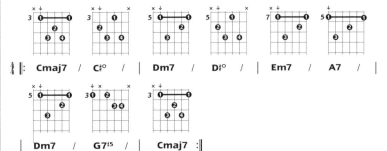

$\frac{4}{4}$ ‖:   Cmaj7 / C♯° / | Dm7   / D♯° / | Em7 / A7 / |

236

| Dm7   / G7♭5 / | Cmaj7 :‖

Jazz 2

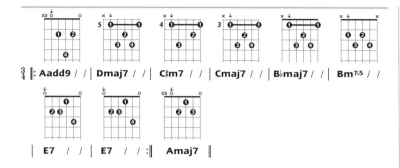

WEB TIPS

The internet offers many more chords and chord diagrams, and you can also go online to find tabs, lyrics, and anything else you need. Here are some suggestions for informative websites. Enjoy!

- www.looknohands.com/chordhouse

- www.gootar.com

- www.thecipher.com

- www.chordbook.com

- www.guitarchords247.com

- www.e-chords.com

- www.911tabs.com

- www.ultimate-guitar.com

- www.guitaretab.com

- www.mxtabs.net

Essential Data

In the event of your equipment being stolen or lost, or if you decide to sell it, it's useful to have all the relevant data at hand. Here are two pages to make those notes. For the insurance, for the police or just for yourself.

INSURANCE

Company:

Phone: Email:

Agent:

Phone: Email:

Policy no.:   Premium:

INSTRUMENTS AND ACCESSORIES

Make and model:

Serial number: Value:

Specifications:

Date of purchase:

Bought at:

Phone: Email:

Make and model:

Serial number: Value:

Specifications:

Date of purchase:

Bought at:

Phone: Email:

Make and model:

Serial number: Value:

Specifications:

Date of purchase:

Bought at:

Phone: Email:

238

STRINGS

You're happy with the strings you're using, but somehow you've forgotten what brand, series or gauge they were, or when you put them on...

Make:	Type:	Gauge/Tension:	Date:

Index

Please check out the glossary on pages 184-188 for additional definitions of the terms used in this book.

240

241

The Tipbook Series

Did you like this Tipbook? There are also Tipbooks for your fellow band or orchestra members! The Tipbook Series features various books on musical instruments, including the singing voice, in addition to Tipbook Music on Paper, Tipbook Amplifiers and Effects, and Tipbook Music for Kids and Teens – a Guide for Parents.

Every Tipbook is a highly accessible and easy-to-read compilation of the knowledge and expertise of numerous musicians, teachers, technicians, and other experts, written for musicians of all ages, at all levels, and in any style of music. Please check www.tipbook.com for up to date information on the Tipbook Series!

All Tipbooks come with Tipcodes that offer additional information, sound files and short movies at www.tipbook.com

Instrument Tipbooks

All instrument Tipbooks offer a wealth of highly accessible, yet well-founded information on one or more closely related instruments. The first chapters of each Tipbook explain the very basics of the instrument(s), explaining all the parts and what they do, describing what's involved in learning to play, and indicating typical instrument prices. The core chapters, addressing advanced players as well, turn you into an instant expert on the instrument. This knowledge allows you to make an informed purchase and get the most out of your instrument. Comprehensive chapters on maintenance, intonation, and tuning are also included, as well a brief section on the history, the family, and the production of the instrument.

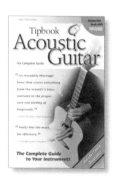

Tipbook Acoustic Guitar – $14.95

Tipbook Acoustic Guitar explains all of the elements that allow you to recognize and judge a guitar's timbre, performance, and playability, focusing on both steel-string and nylon-string instruments. There are chapters covering the various types of strings and their characteristics, and there's plenty of helpful information on changing and cleaning strings, on tuning and maintenance, and even on the care of your fingernails.

243

Tipbook Amplifiers and Effects – $14.95

Whether you need a guitar amp, a sound system, a multi-effects unit for a bass guitar, or a keyboard amplifier, *Tipbook Amplifiers and Effects* helps you to make a good choice. Two chapters explain general features (controls, equalizers, speakers, MIDI, etc.) and figures (watts, ohms, impedance, etc.), and further chapters cover the specifics of guitar amps, bass amps, keyboard amps, acoustic amps, and sound systems. Effects and effect units are dealt with in detail, and there are also chapters on microphones and pickups, and cables and wireless systems.

Tipbook Cello – $14.95

Cellists can find everything they need to know about their instrument in *Tipbook Cello*. The book gives you tips on how to select an instrument and choose a bow, tells you all about the various types of strings and rosins, and gives you helpful tips on the maintenance and tuning of your instrument. Basic information on electric cellos is included as well!

Tipbook Clarinet – $14.95

Tipbook Clarinet sheds light on every element of this fascinating instrument. The knowledge presented in this guide makes trying out and selecting a clarinet much easier, and it turns you into an instant expert on offset and in-line trill keys, rounded or French-style keys, and all other aspects of the instrument. Special chapters are devoted to reeds (selecting, testing, and adjusting reeds), mouthpieces and ligatures, and maintenance.

Tipbook Electric Guitar and Bass Guitar – $14.95

Electric guitars and bass guitars come in many shapes and sizes. *Tipbook Electric Guitar and Bass Guitar* explains all of their features and characteristics, from neck profiles, frets, and types of wood to different types of pickups, tuning machines, and — of course — strings. Tuning and advanced do-it-yourself intonation techniques are included.

Tipbook Drums – $14.95

A drum is a drum is a drum? Not true — and *Tipbook Drums* tells you all the ins and outs of their differences, from the type of wood to the dimensions of the shell, the shape of the bearing edge, and the drum's hardware. Special chapters discuss selecting drum sticks, drum heads, and cymbals. Tuning and muffling, two techniques a drummer must master to make the instrument sound as good as it can, are covered in detail, providing step-by-step instructions.

Tipbook Flute and Piccolo – $14.95

Flute prices range from a few hundred to fifty thousand dollars and more. *Tipbook Flute and Piccolo* tells you how workmanship, materials, and other elements make for different instruments with vastly different prices, and teaches you how to find the instrument that best suits your or your child's needs. Open-hole or closed-hole keys, a B-foot or a C-foot, split-E or donut, inline or offset G? You'll be able to answer all these questions — and more — after reading this guide.

Tipbook Keyboard and Digital Piano – $14.95

Buying a home keyboard or a digital piano may find you confronted with numerous unfamiliar terms. *Tipbook Keyboard and Digital Piano* explains all of them in a very easy-to-read fashion — from hammer action and non-weighted keys to MIDI, layers and splits, arpeggiators and sequencers, expression pedals and multi-switches, and more, including special chapters on how to judge the instrument's sound, accompaniment systems, and the various types of connections these instruments offer.

Tipbook Music for Kids and Teens – a Guide for Parents – $14.95

How do you inspire children to play music? How do you inspire them to practice? What can you do to help them select an instrument, to reduce stage fright, or to practice effectively? What can you do to make practice fun? How do you reduce sound levels and

prevent hearing damage? These and many more questions are dealt with in *Tipbook Music for Kids and Teens – a Guide for Parents and Caregivers*. The book addresses all subjects related to the musical education of children from pre-birth to pre-adulthood.

Tipbook Music on Paper – $14.95

Tipbook Music on Paper – Basic Theory offers everything you need to read and understand the language of music. The book presumes no prior understanding of theory and begins with the basics, explaining standard notation, but moves on to advanced topics such as odd time signatures and transposing music in a fashion that makes things really easy to understand.

Tipbook Piano – $14.95

Choosing a piano becomes a lot easier with the knowledge provided in *Tipbook Piano*, which makes for a better understanding of this complex, expensive instrument without going into too much detail. How to judge and compare piano keyboards and pedals, the influence of the instrument's dimensions, different types of cabinets, how to judge an instrument's timbre, the difference between laminated and solid wood soundboards, accessories, hybrid and digital pianos, and why tuning and regulation are so important: Everything is covered in this handy guide.

Tipbook Saxophone – $14.95

At first glance, all alto saxophones look alike. And all tenor saxophones do too — yet they all play and sound different from each other. *Tipbook Saxophone* discusses the instrument in detail, explaining the key system and the use of additional keys, the different types of pads, corks, and springs, mouthpieces and how they influence timbre and playability, reeds (and how to select and adjust them) and much more. Fingering charts are also included!

Tipbook Trumpet and Trombone, Flugelhorn and Cornet – $14.95

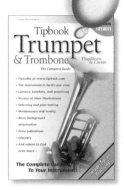

The Tipbook on brass instruments focuses on the smaller horns listed in the title. It explains all of the jargon you come across when you're out to buy or rent an instrument, from bell material to the shape of the bore, the leadpipe, valves and valve slides, and all other elements of the horn. Mouthpieces, a crucial choice for the sound and playability of all brasswinds, are covered in a separate chapter.

Tipbook Violin and Viola – $14.95

Tipbook Violin and Viola covers a wide range of subjects, ranging from an explanation of different types of tuning pegs, fine tuners, and tailpieces, to how body dimensions and the bridge may influence the instrument's timbre. Tips on trying out instruments and bows are included. Special chapters are devoted to the characteristics of different types of strings, bows, and rosins, allowing you to get the most out of your instrument.

Tipbook Vocals – The Singing Voice – $14.95

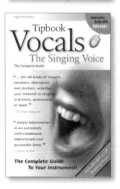

Tipbook Vocals –The Singing Voice helps you realize the full potential of your singing voice. The book, written in close collaboration with classical and non-classical singers and teachers, allows you to discover the world's most personal and precious instrument without reminding you of anatomy class. Topics include breathing and breath support, singing loudly without hurting your voice, singing in tune, the timbre of your voice, articulation, registers and ranges, memorizing lyrics, and more. The main purpose of the chapter on voice care is to prevent problems.

International editions

The Tipbook Series is also available in Spanish, French, German, Dutch, Italian, Swedish, and Chinese. For more information, please visit us at www.tipbook.com.

247

Tipbook Series Music and Musical Instruments

Tipbook Acoustic Guitar
ISBN 978-1-4234-4275-2, HL00332802 − $14.95

Tipbook Amplifiers and Effects
ISBN 978-1-4234-6277-4, HL00332776 − $14.95

Tipbook Cello
ISBN 978-1-4234-5623-0, HL00331904 − $14.95

Tipbook Clarinet
ISBN 978-1-4234-6524-9, HL00332803 − $14.95

Tipbook Drums
ISBN 978-90-8767-102-0, HL00331474 − $14.95

Tipbook Electric Guitar and Bass Guitar
ISBN 978-1-4234-4274-5, HL00332372 − $14.95

Tipbook Flute & Piccolo
ISBN 978-1-4234-6525-6, HL00332804 − $14.95

Tipbook Home Keyboard and Digital Piano
ISBN 978-1-4234-4277-6, HL00332375 − $14.95

Tipbook Music for Kids and Teens
ISBN 978-1-4234-6526-3, HL00332805 − $14.95

Tipbook Music on Paper − Basic Theory
ISBN 978-1-4234-6529-4, HL00332807 − $14.95

Tipbook Piano
ISBN 978-1-4234-6278-1, HL00332777 − $14.95

Tipbook Saxophone
ISBN 978-90-8767-101-3, HL00331475 − $14.95

Tipbook Trumpet and Trombone, Flugelhorn and Cornet
ISBN 978-1-4234-6527-0, HL00332806 − $14.95

Tipbook Violin and Viola
ISBN 978-1-4234-4276-9, HL00332374 − $14.95

Tipbook Vocals − The Singing Voice
ISBN 978-1-4234-5622-3, HL00331949 − $14.95

Check www.tipbook.com for additional information!